# DORM
# LIVING

KNACK

# DORM
# LIVING

## Get the Room—and the Experience—You Want at College

**Casey Lewis**

**Christina Scott, Design Consultant**

*Guilford, Connecticut*
An imprint of Globe Pequot Press

**KNACK®**
**MAKE IT EASY**

Copyright © 2010 by Morris Book Publishing, LLC

ALL RIGHTS RESERVED. No part of this book may be reproduced or transmitted in any form by any means, electronic or mechanical, including photocopying and recording, or by any information storage and retrieval system, except as may be expressly permitted in writing from the publisher. Requests for permission should be addressed to Globe Pequot Press, Attn: Rights and Permissions Department, P.O. Box 480, Guilford, CT 06437.

Knack is a registered trademark of Morris Book Publishing, LLC, and is used with express permission.

Editorial Director: Cynthia Hughes
Editor: Katie Benoit
Project Editor: Tracee Williams
Cover Design: Paul Beatrice, Bret Kerr
Interior Design: Paul Beatrice
Photo Research: Marilyn Zelinsky-Syarto
Front Cover photos courtesy of Jill A. Fox; Bed Bath & Beyond; and © Yuri Arcurs | shutterstock.
Back Cover photo courtesy of Brookstone.
Interior photo credits on pages 238–239.

Library of Congress Cataloging-in-Publication Data

Lewis, Casey, 1987–
  Knack dorm living: get the room, and the experience, you want at college/Casey Lewis; Christina Scott, design consultant.
    p. cm.
  Includes index.
  ISBN 978-1-59921-776-5
  1. Dormitories—United States.  2. Shared housing—United States.
3. College student orientation—United States.  I. Title.

LB3227.5.L49 2010
371.8'710973—dc22
                        2009049560

The following manufacturers/names appearing in *Knack Dorm Living* are trademarks:
3M™, Anthropologie®, Apples to Apples®, Balderdash™, Beanie Babies®, Bissell®, BJ's Wholesale Club®, Catch Phrase®, CHEETOS®, Cheez-It®, Clue®, Costco®, CRAIGSLIST®, Cranium®, eBay®, Energy Star®, Excel®, Facebook®, Fatboy®, Food Network®, FranklinCovey®, Goodwill®, Goo Gone®, GTD®, Guitar Hero®, iPod®, iTunes®, Jenga®, Kleenex®, Mario Kart®, Marshalls®, Mexican Train®, Mint™, Mod Podge®, Moleskine®, Monopoly®, NASCAR®, NETFLIX®, Nintendo®, NyQuil®, Pop-Tarts®, Quicken®, redbox™, Rock Band®, Rolling Stones®, The Salvation Army®, Sam's Club®, Sega®, Skittles®, Sorry!®, Starbucks®, Styrofoam®, Super Mario Bros.™, Swiffer®, T•J•MAXX®, Trivial Pursuit®, Tupperware®, Twinkies®, Twister®, Tylenol®, UNO®, Urban Outfitters®, Velcro®, WD-40®, Wii™, Xbox®, Ziploc®

Printed in China

10 9 8 7 6 5 4 3 2 1

The information in this book is true and complete to the best of our knowledge. All recommendations are made without guarantee on the part of the author or Globe Pequot Press. The author and Globe Pequot Press disclaim any liability in connection with the use of this information

## Dedications

To my adoring (and adorable!) parents who allowed me to spend a school year and two lovely summers living in a dorm.—Casey Lewis

To my mother—my best friend and a wonderful listener. —Christina Scott

## Acknowledgments

An enormous thank you to Katie Benoit and all of the wonderful Knack editors; I could not have done this without you. Christina Scott, you were nothing less than a dorm room miracle worker. Thank you!—Casey Lewis

I'd like to thank Libby Langdon for introducing me to the people at Knack. Your energy and positivity are always an inspiration. I'd also like to thank my father for sending me to college. Without that priceless experience, I would never have been able to work on this book. —Christina Scott

# CONTENTS

# INTRODUCTION

Forget parties—the truth is, college life revolves around the dorm. I have fond memories of my dorm room, but really, this book is a culmination of "things I wish I knew . . ." Prior to college, the only time I had shared a room was at sleep-away camp. Little did I know that my dorm room would be even smaller than my camp cabin (and that the bathrooms were not only "community," but also unisex). Talk about an eye-opener.

For most students, moving to college is the first time away from their parents' nest, so it's essential to create a comfortable home away from home. With creative decorating, meticulous rearranging, and clever organizing, a 12x12 room can become a bona fide abode.

We enlisted the help—and the dorm room—of two college freshmen to apply our favorite design principles to their new college digs (see chapter 19). Emilie and Tessa were friends prior to starting college, but they both had incredibly personal decor preferences.

Emilie couldn't get enough of earthy neutral-colored linens, hippie chic patterned pillows, and an infusion of mementos from her family, while Tessa preferred bright pops of color and frames of photographs galore.

**The Right Room for You:** Choosing the right room for you can make or break the dorm experience. There are many factors to take into consideration when deciding on a dorm. Part of it is luck of the draw, but ultimately your dorm experience relies on cleverly choosing a dorm. Consider all the options: single, double, triple, suite, random roommate, best friend, family acquaintance.

A single sounds a lot more glamorous than it actually is. Sure, having your own space is nice, but much of the college living experience comes with actually living with other people. Sharing a space kind of sounds like a stressful proposition, but in reality, it can be great fun and incredibly valuable.

Emilie and Tessa went with a double suite. They came into college knowing each other, but they quickly expanded their circle of friends thanks to their suite-style bathroom.

**Color Schemes and Decor Themes:** When it comes to decorating a room as small as your dorm room will be, choosing a theme and sticking with it will create style continuity to the whole space.

There's no need to settle on a color scheme with your roommate. If you love red and teal and he or she is into lime green with neon orange (or worse, completely indifferent regarding decorating) take the liberty of choosing colors for your side of the room and run with it.

While Emilie and Tessa had subtly coordinated bedding to begin with—solid-colored comforters with a few bright pillows—their room was largely a blank slate.

**Cheap but Chic:** When you're paying big bucks for a college education, there's no need to take out a loan for dorm decorations, too. For room accents that are as cheap as they are chic, comb through thrift stores, off-price outlets, and sale warehouses.

Leave no garage sale unruffled. If you see one, stop and carefully peek through everything. Imagine old record covers in snazzy new frames and chipped wooden shelves with a fresh coat of paint.

We found most of Emilie and Tessa's new additions at Target and Wal-Mart, with a few key pieces from Crate & Barrel. The takeaway lesson? A room can be completely revamped on a small budget shopping solely at local stores. The key is to think creatively and always keep an eye on the budget.

**Dorm Style Is in the Details:** The right room is more than just the perfectly coordinated bedding or eye-catching rug. To make a dorm room yours, an abundance of unique additions and special decorations that hold personal significance are a must.

Think about things that appeal to your personality. If

sports have always played a big role in your life, stash your soccer balls in a decorative bin instead of dismissing them to under-the-bed storage. If you love fashion, display your most treasured shoes on a shelf or dangle your favorite necklaces from crafty wall hooks.

Because a room's overall decor lies in the details, pay special attention to even the smallest of spaces. Your desk, your closet, even your under-bed area provides an opportunity to express your personal style.

**Stylish Storage:** No residence halls have adequate storage space for all the stuff you'll initially think you need—but once your settle into school, you'll quickly realize you don't need your entire collection of '80s Brat Pack movie posters, your whole set of Super Nintendo video games, or all eighty pairs of high heels.

Once your dorm room is pared down to the real necessities, finding a proper place for everything is essential.

Utilize your under-bed space with sleek storage containers. Opt for bright colors that coordinate with your room's overall color scheme. Even though they'll be stashed under your bed, matching storage bins with your comforter adds a stylish touch.

Emilie and Tessa's under-bed area was completely untapped. Adding a few sets of plastic drawers and matching tubs gave the roommates more room to store out-of-season clothing, cleaning supplies, and extra bed linens.

**Work Hard, Play Hard:** A dorm room must be the ultimate multitasker. It needs to be quiet enough to study in, laidback enough to hang out in, relaxing enough to sleep in, and fun enough to entertain in.

To live up to all of these demands, a bed should double as a place to sleep and a place to sit. A stack of throw pillows decorating your bed can also be used to turn a cold floor into a cozy seating area. A storage cube can also be a card table or a TV perch.

Because we wanted to make sure Emilie and Tessa's room would be ready for work or play, we relegated their school work to desk drawers for safekeeping.

**Looking the Part:** Your dorm room's closet, however humble, is a crucial part of college life. Your college years aren't just for determining your future career—they're also for figuring out your personal style.

Fashion has an enormous affect on first impressions, and college experience is formed by first impression after first impression.

Keeping your wardrobe in tip-top shape will alleviate any temptation to reach for the closest sweats and T-shirts that have been nestled on your floor for days.

By organizing Emilie and Tessa's closets, we put all of their favorite shoes and jeans in constant sight, allowing for easy rotation. Keep your favorites on the forefront, so they're constantly ready to be worn.

It is college, though, so there's a time and a place for sweatpants. Your first class presentation or dining hall date isn't it.

**Dorm Living 101:** Above all, the most important thing about your dorm room is that you're truly comfortable hanging out, studying, sleeping, and just living in it. If the decorations are too elaborate, you won't want to kick back and relax. If the room is too understated, the blank white walls will lull you into a slump.

Create a space that makes you happy just upon entering. Being without your parents for the first time can be a little disorienting, but crafting a home away from home can make the college transition as easy as freshmen year prerequisites.

# SINGLE

## Living alone means lots of room, lots of freedom—and lots of quiet

Although many consider sharing a room with a stranger an integral part of the college experience, it is not a living situation that's right for everyone. The busier your schedule is, the more a single room just makes sense. You can study when you want, sleep when you want, and stay up as late as your chem class demands.

Having a room to yourself also gives you free reign when it comes to decorating your dorm room. Want to cover the walls with Beatles posters? Go for it. Want to turn your humble abode into a polka-dotted palace? No one is stopping you. Want to leave your room as is and luxuriate in the white walls and ho-hum furniture? Well, we might fight you on that one, but there won't be a roommate stopping you.

Another pleasing aspect of single-room living is having the

### Single Dorm Room

- A single dorm room is not, in any sense of the word, spacious, but the entire space is yours.

- Decorating schemes your parents put the kibosh on growing up? No one's stopping you now.

- Let your creativity flow inside the confines of your single dorm by showing your personality through knickknacks and decor.

- "Wallpaper" your walls with posters, frame your band Ts, and stack old textbooks as a bedside table.

### Open-Door Policy

- If you have a single, instill an open-door policy. For a few hours a day, keep your door wide open.

- An open door encourages fellow dorm dwellers to drop in and introduce themselves.

- Forget being lonely living alone—friends will feel free to stop by and say hi if your door's unhinged.

- Another plus? Your neighbors will soon understand that a closed door means you're too busy to chat.

freedom to set your room up exactly as you wish. You can arrange the furniture to your liking—and if you change your mind next week, switching it up doesn't need the approval of anyone else. Don't expect too much extra room; however, you'll most likely be able to fit a handful of extra furniture, like a bookcase, TV stand, or even a cozy lounge chair.

## YELLOW LIGHT

Going to a new school where you know very few people can be an enriching, albeit overwhelming, experience. For those with shy tendencies, living alone may not be the best option out there. Consider living with a family friend, a friend of a friend, or even an acquaintance introduced through summer welcome programs.

## *Making the Most of Your Space*

- Since you'll be enjoying a semester of peace and quiet, create a calm setting to study and relax.

- Set aside your desk for studying, and delegate your bed for unwinding time.

- You won't have a roommate around to keep you in check, so you'll be in charge of your own well-being.

- Don't stay up all night long. Don't keep your TV buzzing all night. And don't blast the music at 6 a.m. You do have neighbors, you know?

### Meeting People

- Make a point to get out and meet people.

- Broadening your horizons—outside of your room—is even more important because you're living alone.

- Join clubs, organize study groups, hang out in common areas, and get involved any way you can (which shouldn't be hard—opportunities abound on campus).

- Smile. College is a new experience for everyone, so showing a friendly face will get you far.

1

# DOUBLE

## Living with a friend (or a foe) is a valuable learning experience in college

The double room is by far the most common dorm living scenario, and for good reason. Sharing a room with only one other person allows for reasonable space, realistic ground rules, and a real built-in buddy. You will learn a lot about yourself while you're learning about someone else. When sharing a 10x10 room for a year, you might, in fact, learn more than you will in a whole semester of freshman year English class.

The key to sharing such a small space is to define your own area, and really let your personality shine through your dorm room. Although this is a temporary home—and certainly not the bedroom of your youth—it's essential to turn that

*Double Dorm Room*

- The way you arrange your double room can make all the difference in your dorm lifestyle.

- On move-in day, set your alarm extra early. Moving in before your roommate guarantees the upper hand

- for deciding on a "side," choosing top or bottom if bunked, and rearranging to your liking.

- Of course, the two of you should eventually mutually decide on a setup that works well for both.

**Double Dorm Blueprint**

- Back-to-back desks give each inhabitant a surprisingly private study nook and office area.

- Pushing the back of your desk against the head of your bed creates a nice makeshift headboard and nightstand.

- When in doubt, bunk the beds. As long as each of you is comfortable sharing your sleeping quarters, the room's floor space will double in size.

white-walled room into a place of comfort and enjoyment for both you and your roommate.

Roommates will not define your college experience, but having a great one will significantly enhance those first few months. Pay close attention to the personality surveys your university distributes with housing information; many will go to great lengths to place you with a like-minded student.

## YELLOW LIGHT

Just like you won't be transforming your dorm room into an HGTV-worthy dwelling, you can't turn a terrible roommate into a great one. If your roommate is affecting your well-being, don't think twice about contacting the residence hall coordinator. The dorm authorities will be more than willing to swap your room assignment. A roommate should never hinder your studies, hurt your grades, or harm your sanity.

## *Merits of Lofting*

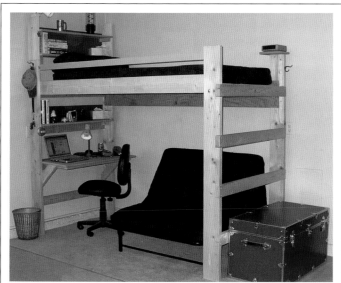

- Many universities have regulations against lofting beds, but if you can get away with it (that is, if the rules allow), lofts are a dorm room's best friend.

- A fully lofted bed can accommodate a desk, arm-chair, or futon underneath your sleeping quarters.

- Can't loft it? Raising a dorm bed to the highest rung can make a serious difference for storage space.

- Many beds go high enough to stash sets of drawers, short bookcases, and mini-fridges.

## *Experiencing Dorm Bathrooms*

- Living in a dorm with a dorm-style bathroom is actually quite convenient. You never have to clean it yourself. Unfortunately, the pampering ends there.

- Dorm-style bathrooms feature a handful of stalls, sinks, and showers. Depending on how many

each floor has, you may have to wait your turn or simply avoid high-traffic times altogether.

- Don't fret about sharing a bathroom with fifty floor-mates. The water's always hot, the stalls are usually clean, and the faces are typically friendly.

# SUITE

A suite-style dorm room promises more space . . . and more people to share with

If the limited space of traditional dorm rooms puts a cramp on your style, consider this roomier setting. Suite-style dorm rooms typically feature a handful of double or triple bedrooms connected to a common room. When it comes to roommates (and rooms), more really is merrier. Not only will you have a handful of built-in friends, but you'll also have extra resources

as far as electronics, appliances, and supplies go.

The sweetest thing about suite-style dorm rooms is that they often include kitchens, living rooms, and dining areas. You'll have a similar setup to an actual apartment without the inconvenience of seeking out off-campus housing. Suites allow students to be completely self-reliant; the extra space for studying,

## Suite-Style Dorm Room

- Suites tout larger bedrooms, along with a generous common room and other amenities that traditional dorm rooms don't have.

- Sofas, tables, chairs, and alcove kitchens are often included in a suite, which makes it ideal for upperclassmen.

- If you're a freshman with a heart set on suite living, sign up early.

- What they don't have is adequate storage space. With four people to two bunk beds, under-the-bed storage is hard to come by.

*Suite-Style Blueprint*

- Suites have more floor space, but they also have more residents per room, which translates to smaller spaces per person.

- Because your bed is your territory, it should be more than just a place to sleep. Make your bunk your own domain.

- View your bed as your own "room" and take advantage of every inch.

- The ceiling, the wall, and bedding are all opportunities to display your style.

cooking, and hanging out will prove indispensable.

The luxury of a living area promises that you'll always have somewhere to escape to if you need a change of scenery. Roommate needs a nap after pulling an all-nighter? Take your studies to the next room. Best friend coming over? Politely ask your roommate for a little privacy, and promise to show him or her the same respect.

Suites are a lot of fun because there's always someone around and something going on.

····· YELLOW LIGHT ·····

If you're easily distracted, suite-style dorm rooms may not be for you. Interruptions go hand-in-hand with more room-mates, and quiet time is impossible to find. Either avoid suite-style living or invest in a high-quality pair of earplugs. If you thrive being surrounded by others and feel inspired by conversations and interactions, a suite-style dorm room is for you.

## Suite Bathroom

- Sharing a bathroom with four to six other people is much more low-key than elbowing through an entire floor for a spot in the shower.

- The only downside is that the residents are usually in charge of cleaning the bath-room in their own suite. You know what that means— bathroom-cleaning duties!

- Split the cost of supplies and trade off tasks. Be sure to check with your resident coordinator to find out if toilet paper is included.

## Suite Kitchen

- A dorm suite kitchen won't be much bigger than a closet, and it won't feature any fancy appliances, but it will be the perfect place to flex your culinary skills.

- The luxury of a kitchen comes with responsibilities: Take care of your own gro-ceries and clean your own dishes and messes.

- Make the most of your amenities and invest in a cookbook.

- When you're tired of caf-eteria food, which happens faster than you'd think, that stove top will be a lifesaver.

# COMMON ROOM

An all-purpose area that acts as a living room, study hall, and hang out all in one

The dorm's eponymous common room, often found anchoring two, three, or four dorm rooms, can be a great place to spend time just steps from your room. The furniture is usually nothing to fuss over: a few standard cushion chairs, a coffee table, and a couch if you're lucky. But the generous space of a common room allows for a little additional furniture and a lot of additional fun.

When it comes to such a clean slate, a few decorations go a long way. Look for colorful touches to brighten up the entire room. Patterned pillows, throw blankets, a nice green plant will boost the decoration without breaking the budget.

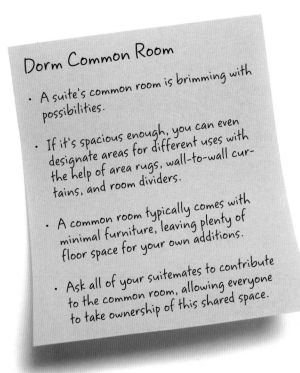

Dorm Common Room

- A suite's common room is brimming with possibilities.

- If it's spacious enough, you can even designate areas for different uses with the help of area rugs, wall-to-wall curtains, and room dividers.

- A common room typically comes with minimal furniture, leaving plenty of floor space for your own additions.

- Ask all of your suitemates to contribute to the common room, allowing everyone to take ownership of this shared space.

*Decorate with Draperies*

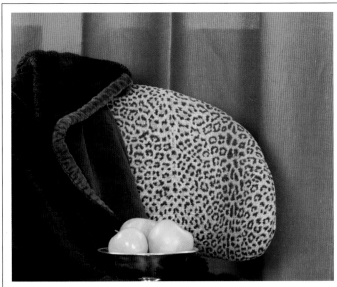

- Bright draperies can make all the difference in common rooms.

- Not only do they provide privacy, they bring tons of color to an otherwise drab room.

- Chip in to purchase inexpensive curtains, or simply buy a compression rod and a few yards of bright fabric.

- If you can't turn fabric into homespun curtains, enlist the help of a friend (or helpful mom) who has basic sewing skills.

A common room is a space intended to be shared, so choose universally appealing decor. Since this is the first time you and your suitemates have been away from home for an extended period of time, any accessories reminiscent of home will be much appreciated.

Ask everyone to pitch in a few pieces from their own homes, and before you know it, your humble common room will begin to resemble a lovely haven. Blankets, tapestries, and flat sheets can transform ordinary furniture into extraordinary features.

## Pillows Provide Comfort

- You don't need to buy blankets and pillows specifically for your common room.

- Stow any extras in the common room for drop-in friends and impromptu get-togethers.

- You can find pretty inexpensive throw pillows. If you don't have change to spare, they can be crafted out of anything from vintage silk scarves to high school band Ts to fabric remnants.

- Blankets can be as no-frills as your pillows. Hand-me-down quilts, wool throws, and big squares of flannel fabric are perfectly homey.

············· YELLOW ● LIGHT ·············

Many traditional single- and two-person dorm rooms do not have attached common rooms but instead offer common areas every few floors. These don't offer the same amount of freedom as in-suite common rooms, but they do offer a nice reprieve from the confines of your own room. Ask for an okay from the residence hall coordinator to have a decorating day to paint the walls, draw a mural, or hang posters.

### Study Hall or Student Lounge?

- Communicate with your suitemates about the purpose of your common room.

- Consider drafting an informal schedule. For example, hang out with friends through the afternoon, then designate quiet time for study hall during the evening hours.

- If you're planning to invite friends or classmates over for a specific time, run it by your suitemates in advance to put the kibosh on any conflict of interests.

# APARTMENT STYLE
Opt for a little more space to insert your personal style

Some universities prohibit living off campus during the first year of college, but still many colleges allow it, and a handful even offer off-campus apartments as an alternative housing option. This is a great choice for undergrads with intensive majors like pre-med, pre-law, and engineering. It's also a nice option for students looking to save money. No matter how no-frills dorms may seem, they aren't cheap to live in.

Living away from campus allows you to discover a community apart from the university. A rule of thumb is that the farther from campus you venture, the more affordable apartments are. Look into established neighborhoods and up-and-coming areas for environments conducive to students.

Don't stray too far from school, however. Biking distance is preferable, and walking distance is even better. Go any

### The Apartment Alternative

- A studio apartment is an affordable option, especially if you prefer living alone or don't mind sharing a small space.

- Basement apartments are also inexpensive. Plus they can be perfectly private if you anticipate intense studying.

- Three- and four-bedroom apartments can replicate dorm living away from campus—and they have the luxury of additional privacy.

- Wherever you choose to live will be smaller than your previous space, so smart decorating is a must.

### Apartments: A Life of Luxury

- Skipping dorm living means skipping the dorm basics, like plastic bins and other disposable decor.

- Take strides to make purchases that will last throughout your young adulthood; consult your parents on what's worth saving for and scrimping on.

- A comfortable bed, quality desk, and stylish couch are worth the splurge.

- To avoid going broke furnishing your first home away from home, hunt through vintage and thrift stores to find previously loved gems.

farther, and you'll have to deal with daily driving and hectic on-campus parking (which often translates to parking passes, metered parking, or monumental parking tickets). Public buses are a better option for off-campus students, but still requiring waiting at the bus stop, which doesn't exactly encourage regular class attendance. To ensure that moving to an apartment won't lessen your college experience, spend adequate time on campus.

## MAKE IT EASY

Heading to college close to home? Living with parents can be an inexpensive short-term option. This alternative allows you to save some cash the first semester or two. In order to get the full college experience, however, make a point to spend some extra time on campus, sign up for student organizations, and plan on living with fellow classmates at least a few of your university years.

## *Getting Around Town*

- Living off campus makes organization of the utmost importance. When you live in the dorm, you can oversleep and run to class.

- Keep a few transportation options on hand: Biking, driving, and bus passes will make getting around much more manageable.

- The closer to campus you are, the more you'll make it to class.

- Living within biking (or better yet, walking) distance is ideal because you can get around with ease while fitting in exercise.

### The Merits of Apartment Alternatives

- Living in the dorm is not "one size fits all." For creative types who thrive on energy and rely on their surroundings for inspiration, residence halls might be a little lacking.

- There are ways around spending a year in a dorm. Some universities only require one semester of resident life, while others provide apartment alternatives as a housing option.

- If you're interested in exploring the apartment option, pay attention to the proximity to campus.

- The closer, the better, especially when you're new to town.

# HOW TO CHOOSE?

## Weighing the positives and negatives can help you pick the perfect living arrangement

When it comes time to decide what kind of dorm room you'll be living in for the next year, take a close look at yourself—and put some thought into the person you hope to be in college. If you aspire to be a social butterfly, a four-person room guarantees study buddies. If you're serious about school and you value alone time, a single room might be more your speed.

Sometimes moving in with a friend from school or an acquaintance from home can make the transition to college easier; on the other hand, going the "random roommate" route can be an exciting way to meet your new best buddy.

Living with your partner in crime from high school might seem like a smart solution, but oftentimes this living scenario

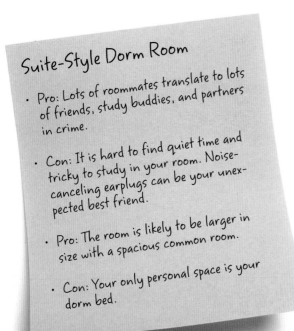

**Suite-Style Dorm Room**

- Pro: Lots of roommates translate to lots of friends, study buddies, and partners in crime.

- Con: It is hard to find quiet time and tricky to study in your room. Noise-canceling earplugs can be your unexpected best friend.

- Pro: The room is likely to be larger in size with a spacious common room.

- Con: Your only personal space is your dorm bed.

*Single Dorm Room*

- Pro: You have as much privacy as you could possibly want.

- Con: You might have too much alone time, especially if you're shy by nature.

- Pro: You can decorate exactly as you wish, acting on every decor whim.

- Con: You're in charge of footing the bill for everything you need. When you live alone, there's no roommate to split the cost of fridges, TVs, and area rugs.

makes shifting from a high school to a college mind-set more challenging than your first week of finals. Starting fresh can be easier when you're surrounded by new faces.

Give your dorm preferences a lot of thought. A handful of residence halls are still same-sex dorms, but coed dorms are quickly taking over campus. If you aren't comfortable sleeping and showering on the same floor as the opposite sex, opt out of these.

## Double Dorm Room

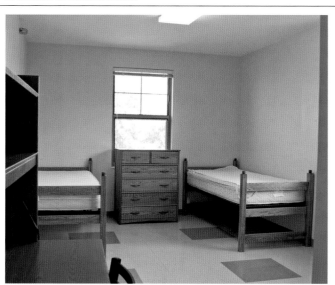

- Pro: You share your space with only one other person, giving you more independence—and storage.

- Con: If things don't click with your only roommate, you don't have anyone else in the room to turn to—other than the residence hall advisor to beg and plead for a room change.

- Pro: You can bunk your beds and double your floor space.

- Con: You have the same sleeping arrangement you had in summer camp in fifth grade.

### A Mid-Year Move

- Sometimes a seemingly ideal living situation just doesn't work out.

- Don't just grin and bear it; take control and change it. A mid-year move is a nice option if you get antsy after spending the semester in a certain room of a certain dorm with a certain roommate.

- You don't owe it to your roommate to explain your desire for a dorm-room switch. Simply explain that you thrive on change and would like to try something different.

# PACKING UP

Those people who pack for vacation the night before takeoff have never moved to college

You may be tempted to pack up your entire room to ship off to school, but packing with such a heavy hand will result in a dorm room so stuffed you won't be able to find your backpack. Instead, determine the necessities and box them up in an organized manner, allowing for optimal unpacking.

Classic brown boxes work like a charm, because all it takes is a quick Sharpie scrawl to label with care. Ziplock bags, now available as big as trash-bag size, can be resealed again and again, preventing spillage and encouraging double-checking. Even better, they can be discarded after a use or two because they're easy on the wallet. Milk crates are stackable, see-through, and colorful; they're convenient enough

## Boxing It Up

winter clothes

- Classic brown boxes are as useful as ever. Not only are they inexpensive, they're ecofriendly—and very reliable, at that.

- If packed correctly, sturdy cardboard can withstand unwieldy objects and lots of weight.

- They're also brilliant for transporting knickknacks that might get lost in the big move.

- Use brown boxes for any breakables, and pack tightly with foam peanuts, bubble plastic, and lots of duct tape. And don't forget to label!

## Lugging the Extras

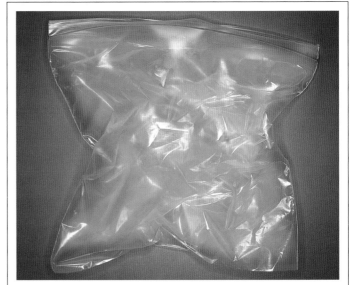

- Tossing everything into a handful of gallon-size trash bags is an easy way to pack—until you try to unpack and realize you can't even find anything.

- Oversize ziplock bags are a tidy alternative to the pack-rat route.

- Great for clothes and sheets, trash bag–size ziplocks have an airtight seal to save much-needed moving space.

- Best of all, they come with a convenient label large enough for a detailed rundown of the contents.

to use for the big move and cute enough to keep around the room for storage purposes.

A rule of thumb: If you can't pack it all into one car, it probably won't pack into your side of the dorm room either. It's better to start off small, only carting the necessities to your new home. You can have Mom and Dad send anything else once you have the chance to assess whether you really need it.

## *Crating Your Stuff*

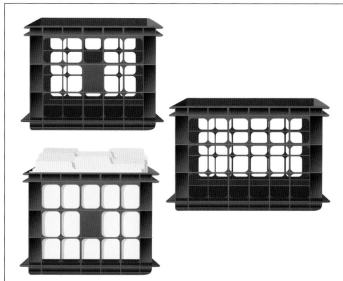

- Use milk crates to cart all of your bigger possessions. Toss in athletic equipment, beloved novels, your wear-everywhere shoes, and anything else that won't slip through the cracks.

- Although you might be tempted to toss this blanket in with that baseball mitt, keep things as orderly as possible to take the puzzle out of unpacking.

- Buy milk crates in a few of your favorite colors and organize by shade: blue for bedding, orange for office supplies.

## *Transporting Your Wardrobe*

- Garment bags take the guesswork out of transferring dresses, suits, and dry clean–only clothes to and from school (and, eventually, to and from the dry cleaners).

- T-shirts, shorts, and jeans, on the other hand, can be safely tossed into any ol' container.

- Although they're intended for travel, garment bags expertly reduce the space needed for your closet's larger items.

- Stow your winter coats and scarves in one during the off-season, then stash your sundresses later in the year.

# DORM TOOL KIT
Everything you need to fix dorm furnishings and accidents quickly

How much can you possibly need for a 12 x 12 room that's already furnished to the brim? A lot, apparently. Over the course of the year, things will break—everything from chair legs (hence the duct tape) to, well, your roommate's leg (hence the first aid kit).

Even if you've never used a hammer in your life, a few beginner tools are helpful to have on hand. While you're buying all of the obvious dorm necessities, toss a compact tool kit into the cart. You'll be surprised just how often you reach for that screwdriver.

Many universities don't allow residents to hammer holes into the walls, which is where adhesive stickies come in handy. Available in many sizes and shapes, these indispensable bonding agents can attach anything you could dream

## Tape: The Tool of Champions

- If it's broken, duct tape will fix it. Wobbly desk chairs, damaged desk drawers, and textbooks with covers dangling by a thread can benefit from the tough tape.

- Secure extension cords and electronic cables in place with duct tape to avoid trips and trips.

- You didn't hear it from us, but duct tape is a prankster's best friend, flawlessly taping doors shut, creating impossible mazes, and infuriating your nemesis.

## Sticky Tacky and Other Adhesives

- It's still a mystery how college students survived without removable adhesives. These magical stickies can mount everything from decorative hooks to framed posters to wall organizers.

- Stickable to any surface, spring clips are among the most useful. For decoration

- and organization at once, clip on family photos, school notes, or magazine tear outs.

- Sticky tacky has been a dorm mainstay for the past thirty years, but residence halls are beginning to outlaw the sticky substance because of its oily residue.

of to your walls, your furniture, and your door.

The key is to keep the final move out in mind. Adhesives will come off with a quick flick of the wrist, leaving no residue behind. Duct tape, on the other hand, is not so convenient to remove. Keep the sensitive-adhesive tape around for repairs, but don't use it to put up that poster, because it won't make it down in one piece (and neither will the plaster).

## ZOOM

Since you won't have a resident handyman on call, consult dear ol' Dad on the necessary tools to survive at the dorm. He can tell you everything you need, when to use them, and how to avoid injuries. Accidents do happen, and if that hammer mistakenly hits the wrong nail (as in, your thumbnail), the first aid kit will be a lifesaver.

## Injuries, Accidents, and First Aid

- Accidents happen. Especially when a campus full of kids are away from their parents' watchful eyes for the first time in, well, ever.

- Keep a first aid kit close by for scrapes, sprains, and the odd broken limb. More than likely, you'll find yourself on nurse duty with the nickname of "Mom" for the rest of the semester, but at least you're prepared.

- Never keep prescription meds in your first aid kit. You don't want your medically prescribed pills to end up in the wrong hands.

## Tool Kit for Beginners

- A small kit equipped with screwdrivers, hammers, and a variety of nails will serve you well through college.

- Lofting a bed is much harder work than it seems, and pulling a nail out with the back of a hammer is much simpler than using your own nails.

- If you don't know a screwdriver from a wrench, make fast friends with a floormate who is well versed in tool speak.

- Come to an understanding— he can help you with dorm room upkeep; you can help him with calculus homework.

15

# WHAT TO BRING

A few of your favorite things bring the familiar comforts of home to a brand-new room

Your dorm room will be your home away from home, but don't just zap your old stuff to your new digs. You'll be walking into school expecting a fresh start, and that carries over to the dorm, too.

Go through your room with a very skeptical eye. Only bring things you know you'll need, and set aside stuff that will be needed later in the year. Ask your parents to send what you need when you need it instead of bringing everything you might possibly use during the year. Don't be a pack rat.

Speaking of pack rats, if you have a history of keeping everything that's ever landed in your possession, packing for college is the perfect time to clear your room at home.

## Family Photographs

- Print out a stack of your favorite photographs before leaving home and put them in a prominent place once you move in.

- Seeing your family and closest friends smiling back at you in your new life will be unspeakably comforting.

- Dig through antiques stores, corner boutiques, and your parents' basement for frames, then redecorate them as you see fit.

- A lot of acrylic paint and a little handiwork goes a long way.

## Spare Change

- Humble rolls of quarters are a necessity to survive freshman year.

- Whether you're living large with a trust fund or you're up to your ears in student loans, spare change will save the day.

- Laundry and parking

- meters require coins, and your college life requires both of these luxuries.

- Dorms are dotted with vending machines full of guilty pleasures like cans of soda and candy bars. Save these cheap thrills for emergency study sessions.

Get rid of everything you no longer need. Your grade school softball cleats? No longer useful. Notebooks from junior high science? That's not going to boost your upper-level chemistry grade.

If you find yourself longing for home, reminders from your parent's house will silence those lingering "I miss Mom" feelings. Be prepared for a touch of homesickness during finals, and remedy the nostalgia with framed pictures, homey knickknacks, and that stuffed animal you've slept with every night for the past fifteen years.

## ZOOM

American novelist John Cheever once said "Homesickness is nothing. Fifty percent of the people in the world are homesick all the time." Homesickness, defined as "longing for home and family while absent from them," was added to the Webster Dictionary in 1756. Proven ways to stave off homesickness include staying busy, exploring the new environment, and remaining optimistic.

## Pieces of Home

- Covering every inch of your wall with photos from home isn't visually pleasing or particularly healthy.

- A few reminders of home will stave off nostalgia with style.

- Grandma's quilt, Dad's favorite record cover, and Mom's old jewelry box (is that aiming too high?) are sweet mementos that will add a little something to your dorm room.

- Remember to ask permission before lifting possessions from your parents' home if you ever want to be welcomed home.

## Leaving Clothes Behind

- Whatever you do, do not bring your entire wardrobe. You won't wear half of it, and you certainly won't have room for all of it.

- Weather can't always be predicted, but the size of your closet can. It will be, in a word, tiny.

- Swap your fall clothes for winter gear during Thanksgiving break, then grab your warm weather wardrobe around spring break.

- If unexpected weather hits, consider it an excuse to go shopping.

# WHAT TO BUY

## College shopping can seem overwhelming, but buying the right necessities can help you get off to a great start

Every department store from your hometown to your college town will undoubtedly have a section entirely devoted to "dorm necessities." That doesn't mean you need to buy up the whole division. There are some things you will need to buy (like bedding) and some things you won't (like an industrial-strength paper shredder).

Mom can be a very helpful voice to have around while back-to-school shopping, but well-meaning mothers also have a way of overzealously preparing. It's in their nature. Don't get talked into quart-size coffee makers "just in case," or enough shampoo to last you a year "to be on the safe side." Assure her (and that nagging voice inside your own

### Brand-New Bedding

- Packing bedding is a pain. The fitted sheet never quite folds right, and a comforter takes up more space than an entire wardrobe.

- Hold off on buying bedding until you make the move, or at the very least, keep your new sleep stuff neatly

tucked away in its airtight package.

- Don't forget to wash the new sheets before you sleep—cotton just isn't as soft straight from the store, and it doesn't smell nearly as homey as freshly laundered bedding.

### Bed Lifters

- Bed risers, rack raisers, and unassuming cement blocks can double the storage space underneath your bed, which is beyond beneficial when you understand that under the bed is a dorm's lone place for extra stuff.

- Bed risers add inches, while rack raisers provide more

than two feet.

- Cinder blocks, found at any home improvement store, are an inexpensive way to add height to your bed, offering nearly eight inches.

- Paint cinder blocks—your dorm doesn't need any superfluous gray decor.

head) that you can get what you need when you need it.

Put yourself on a college-shopping budget unless you're okay with going into debt before you even set foot on campus. It's true that you'll need to purchase a lot of stuff, but you should be able to afford everything you need without taking out a loan. Pay attention to prices, pass on things you don't really need, and scrimp where you can.

**ZOOM**

The average college freshman drops well over a thousand bucks on back-to-school shopping. With wise budgeting, you can spend half that and still live like royalty (save the surplus of cash for spring break!). Spend less by buying things as you need them instead of buying everything you think you'll need.

## Under-the-Bed Organization

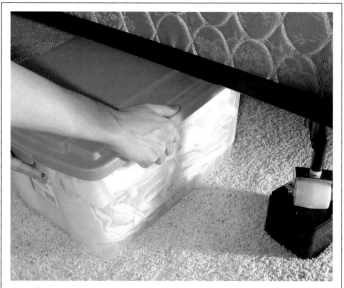

- A dorm bed offers nearly seven feet of untapped space for storage. Make the most of every inch with under-bed organizers.

- When it comes to stowing hampers, drawers, and oversize crates beneath where you sleep, wheels are crucial.

- Mobilizing storage containers takes the misery out of finding a needed textbook or certain sweater.

- Without wheels, your underbed storage will be cramped, dark, and not at all convenient.

## Dealing with Hangers

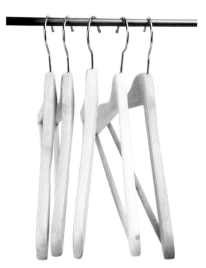

- Closets are a luxury in residence halls, so if you're lucky enough to have one, you must pack wisely.

- No matter how meticulously organized your closet at home is, grabbing clothes from the rack and transporting them on hangers is not the answer.

- Hangers, especially the pesky wire ones, can take hours to untangle. And who wants to spend an hour doing such an unpleasant task when opportunities abound just outside your dorm?

# WHAT TO RENT
## Give your wallet a rest and rent big-ticket items

Universities sympathize with the growing cost of college by offering opportunities to rent big-ticket purchases instead of buying everything your first year requires.

Many kids have Richie Rich fantasies of bedrooms equipped with sugar-stocked minifridges. But the reality of a "fun-size" refrigerator is far less glamorous, and there's no need to buy one to fulfill such a fleeting need. As soon as you move out of

the dorm, you'll be ready for a full-size fridge and the allure of a shoebox freezer will no longer hold the same appeal.

The answer? Rent one. You can rent this, and many temporary necessities like furniture, electronics, and appliances. Rental options are especially abundant in college towns. Sometimes the service is even offered by the residence halls.

### Minirefrigerators

- A minifridge is a must for any college student, and many universities rent out the pint-size appliance to save residents the trouble.

- There are few downsides to renting a fridge, especially since you can split the one-time cost with your roommate so easily.

- It's tough to damage a minifridge, so this is a reasonably low-risk appliance to rent. Just make sure you don't have any unsightly leaks!

### Renting Electronics

- Rather than purchasing the doodads to accompany a TV, consider renting them.

- DVRs, DVD players, and video game systems can be checked out by the month.

- Chances are either you or your roommate will have a spare TV set laying around. If not, TVs can also be rented, but it's often cheaper just to buy a no-frills set.

- High-tech home theater systems are also available on a limited basis; if you and your friends have a much-anticipated season finale coming up, it might be worth the splurge.

If your college doesn't offer any services or special deals, look into local renting centers. These stores carry top appliance brands and will be willing to rent for short- or long-term periods of time.

Another option for temporary essentials is to buy gently used goods by reading classified ads and searching through online classified Web sites. They won't last forever, but they will get you through freshmen year.

······· YELLOW ● LIGHT ·······

Before you rent, do a price check. In some cases it's actually cheaper to buy small appliances than it is to rent. When it comes to things like basic TV sets and miniature refrigerators, you might be better off making the purchase even if you just use it through college. If you end up buying a mini-fridge for the year, look into selling it to an incoming freshman the following year.

## Off-Campus Storage

- Renting a storage unit makes sense for out-of-state students, especially if four years in college warrant four different residences.

- Furniture and out-of-season clothes can be stowed out of sight until needed for far less than the price of shipping.

- College towns rent storage units for very little money, but big city–bound students are better off simply paring back on belongings.

- Some schools offer storage options worth looking into, especially for over summer break.

**Renter's Remorse**

- No matter what you're planning to rent, a contract will be required. Pay very close attention to the fine print of this contract.

- Like when your professor hands out an exam, read carefully, check over your answers, and know exactly what you're turning in.

- Sometimes rental contracts include automatic renewals and over-the-top late fees. This doesn't mean the company isn't trustworthy, but you need to be aware of what you're committing to.

# WHAT TO LEAVE

Saying "goodbye" to your family and familiar bedroom and saying "hello" to new digs and a fresh start

So what shouldn't you bring to college? Your entire childhood bedroom, that's what. Leave the high school mementos behind. Your football jersey will not come in handy, nor will your collection of yearbooks. College is a new chapter of life, and revisiting who won "Most Likely to Succeed" will not boost your collegiate success.

Don't bring along your most treasured knickknacks. Mom's crystal vase will look mighty nice on your dresser until it gets misplaced or accidentally broken. Bringing excessively nice things to college will get you noticed, but not for the right reasons. Plus, residence hall coordinators won't have a whole lot of sympathy for the kid who got his grandfather's third-

## Candles

- There are plenty of alternatives to a scented candle for a room that smells less than fresh.

- Because they're such a serious fire hazard, even the sweet-smelling candle is not something worth bending the rules for.

- Wall plug-ins and reed diffusers can mask unwashed dishes, unwashed clothes, even unwashed students (but showering is still necessary).

- Buy home-fragrance spray. Like perfume for your dorm, a spritz freshens up your space in no time.

## Forbidden Food Appliances

- Toaster ovens, hot pots, slow cookers, and countertop grills are just a few of the kitchen appliances on the growing list of forbidden foodie favorites.

- Don't even try to sneak something in. Most dorms and dining halls are stocked with an array of appliances for your cooking whims.

- However, if your dorm does allow toaster ovens, definitely add one to your ever-expanding list of must-haves. These portable stoves whip up warm meals in a flash.

generation family crest stolen; some things just don't belong in a dorm room.

That goes for your pet, too. Even if you're sure no one will notice your kitten's purring or your puppy's temperamental growls, you'll never get away with it.

Many kitchen appliances aren't allowed in dorm rooms, but the majority of dorms give microwaves the okay and, really, what more does a college student need?

**ZOOM**

Pay close attention to the things prohibited in your dorm. It might seem harmless to sneak a hot plate or a lava lamp into your room, but resident hall coordinators have the right to take a peek in your room at any given moment, and your beloved possession will promptly be confiscated. The things that are forbidden are forbidden for a reason—hot plates and toaster ovens are huge fire hazards.

**MOVING IN**

## Cherished Treasures and Valuables

- You're likely to have acquired a few treasured possessions by the time you go off to college, but think twice about bringing those valuables.

- No matter how diligent you are about locking the door behind you, friends are in and out of dorm rooms all day, and things have a way of going missing.

- Expensive purses, jewelry, and knickknacks are just not dorm friendly.

- Leave your most precious items at home freshman year; they're much more suited to apartment living.

## Painting Your Dorm

- Residence halls are surprisingly flexible about allowing residents to repaint their rooms.

- Universities usually require approval regarding paint colors, but they'll often throw in a can or two of free paint if you choose a pre-approved color.

- Maneuvering around a dorm room to repaint is a lot of work, and keep in mind that you might have to paint over it come summertime.

- Before you begin consider whether freshly covered walls are worth such a time commitment.

# DECOR SCHEME

## Learn your design sensibilities, from prints to patterns, colors to shades

Deciphering a decor scheme is similar to setting a grade goal in class: It's a work in progress. Touch base with your roommate to find out if you have similar design sensibilities and want to collaborate on your dorm room, or simply select a scheme for your side of the room.

Once you define what you want your dorm decor to be, keep your eyes peeled for embellishments and add-ons throughout the semester. Perhaps you have been inspired by a recent trip to the country? Look for homespun ornamentation, like stripes, patchwork, and brief-yet-bold touches of color. Maybe you want your room to resemble that really cool architecture firm you worked at last summer. Stick with

### Shopping for Housewares

- You probably won't have the budget to buy every pretty thing in your favorite home decor catalog, but use it as a muse.

- Tear out any pages that inspire you. The great thing about DIY is that it can really be done yourself.

- You don't have to be an interior decorator to polka dot your walls or line your drawers with fancy fabric.

- Pick and choose a few pricey pieces to mix in with your discount and thrift store finds.

### Choosing a Color Scheme

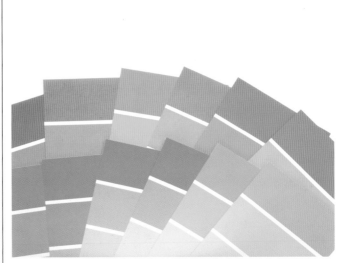

- Matchy-matchy is over-rated, but color coordination adds a sophisticated continuity to the room.

- If you and your roommate can agree on favorite shades from the color wheel, choose your bedding, wall decorations, and rugs accordingly.

- Only go along with a certain color scheme if you truly love it. After college you'll have no use for a lavender carpet unless you adore the color purple.

- And a bright pink bedspread? Only the sunniest student can pull off such a wide-eyed piece.

metallic accents, minimalist storage containers, and simple shapes.

Whatever you do, don't come up with a gimmicky theme and decorate your room accordingly. This isn't a school dance. "Under the stars" or "island in the sun" does not a decor scheme make. At the same time, don't choose two garish colors as the basis for your dorm decorating. Pink and green are both lovely colors, but just as you would never wear the two shades head to toe, you shouldn't decorate your room in them from dresser to desk.

ROOMING

## Matching Bedding

- Buying the same bedspread as your roommate is kind of like wearing the same outfit as your best friend—cute, but only before the age of five.

- If you're set on matching, buy the same solid-colored comforter. That way you can match while still making the bed yours by adding charming pillows or cozy throws.

- A similarly patterned duvet in the same color scheme is also a happy compromise that allows you to honor your personal taste and stick with a decor theme.

## Decorative Pillows

- Bright, patterned pillows infuse even more personality than your bedspread will.

- You can scrimp on a comforter and choose the most basic neutral color bedcover, as long as you add a plethora of whimsical pillows.

- Decorative throw pillows can really add up, so consider purchasing a few plain accent pillows and then embellishing or recovering them.

- Everything from silk scarves to high school T-shirts can turn an ordinary cushion into a unique, playful pillow.

25

# CREATING YOUR SPACE

## No matter how small, your room is an untapped setting to display personality

When it comes to dorm living, the beauty of your space, no matter how small, is that it's yours. Every surface, every shelf, every corner should be infused with your personality. Instead of dwelling on what you can't do to your dorm room, focus on what you can.

Temporary decor doesn't have to be complicated, but it does require oodles of creativity. Want to polka dot your walls? Cut circle shapes out of colorful card stock and attach them with sticky tack. Want to turn your ho-hum furniture into whimsical assets? Grab a roll of patterned wrapping paper or removable contact sheets and get to work.

Everyone can put his or her stamp on a dorm room, just like

### Photo Clothesline

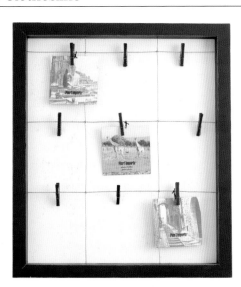

- Do you have more photos than frames? Attach a laundry line to the wall using adhesive eye hooks, then use clothespins to clip on your favorite pictures. This creates a charming wall decoration with minimal effort.

- As you meet new people and make new friends, add new snapshots to your ever-expanding collage.

- This photograph clothesline looks particularly perfect centered over your bed and keeps your treasured photos in constant view.

### Wrapping Paper

- Add color to your drab desk with a roll or two of wrapping paper.

- Simply measure the back boards of the hutch and cut out the cheeriest, shiniest wrapping paper you can find to fit the area. Carefully attach with adhesive stickies and behold your beautiful new desk.

- Mix and match wrapping paper colors and swap patterns as you see fit. Leftovers can be used to brighten up your shelves, too!

everyone has the ability to excel in college. Whatever you do, don't settle for white walls and tile floors. Embellish, decorate, and beautify your dorm just like you would your own apartment. Even something as simple as corkboard covered with your favorite snapshots, magazine tear outs, and letters can make an outstanding difference.

If you can't nail shelves into your walls, use the top shelf of your desk as a mantelpiece for all of your nearest and dearest belongings.

Personality is defined as "distinction or excellence of personal and social traits." How does this translate to decorating? Think about what makes you you: Your interests, your passions, your heritage, and your history should all be included in your decor.

## Sheer Fabric

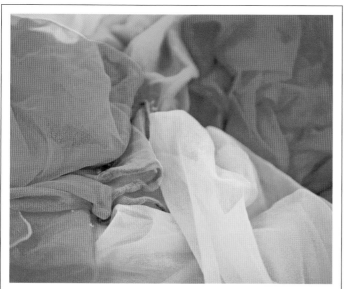

- Purchase swaths of sheer fabric for mere pennies and drape them around your room to create a cozy dwelling.

- Sheer material is the perfect match for your window's dusty miniblinds; simply frame the windowsill with a few hooks and a bough of your favorite fabric.

- Sheer fabric can also stand in for closet doors, room dividers, and decorative wall panels.

- Because this fabric is usually a net-like material, adhesive hooks can be poked directly through the threads.

### Clipboard Decor

- Collect six to eight classic office clipboards, typically found at supply stores for a few bucks a piece.

- Organize them into two rows, then affix them to the wall, leaving several inches of space in between (you can measure and mark before sticking them up).

- Mounting adhesives are ideal—they can withstand the weight of clipboards and will remove with ease.

- Part decoration, part organization: Display exam reminders, memorable mail, and magazine tear outs.

# BUNKING BEDS
## Save space and channel your inner-kid with doubled-up bunk beds

Bunking beds is a brilliant way to save space while maximizing your secrecy. Bunked beds give each resident his or her own little hideaway. It's a win-win situation. The top bunk is tall enough to redeem a little privacy, while the bottom bunk is just begging for a "bedchamber" curtain.

Choosing top or bottom is a win-win situation. On one hand (or one mattress, rather), the birds-eye view bestows more privacy. At the same time, you can't beat the convenience of lying so low to the ground.

Whether you grew up with bunk beds or not, they'll instantly make you feel like a kid again. Come to think of it, living in a dorm is a lot like summer camp. You live in a tiny hut, you meet more people in a week than you have in your entire life, and you have a lot of fun.

### Two Twin Beds

- A dorm room with two twin beds can limit the space for additional furniture.

- Give a lot of thought and imagination to the layout to maximize your floor space.

- Factoring in the requisite desk and dresser, couches, lounge chairs, and coffee tables are out of the question unless you bunk your beds.

- You'll sacrifice a little personal space (i.e., under your bed), but you'll have extra privacy and won't have to be under the watchful eye of your roommate every hour of the day.

### One Bunk Bed

- The same room with bunked beds looks bigger and touts up to two times the floor space.

- The only downside to bunking up is forgoing your under-the-bed storage space. This can be easily remedied by adding a set of shelves or a slim, tall dresser—after all, you'll have the space to spare.

- Question whether it's worth the trade off: extra furniture for fewer storage spots.

## Bed Curtains

- Whether you have the top or bottom bunk, bed curtains will give you more privacy than you ever dreamed of while living in the dorm.

- Pieces of fabric will make any simple dorm furniture look impossibly fancy.

- If you have the lower level, invest in a compression rod and hang a piece of fabric or shortened curtains across the bunk.

- If you're up top, use adhesive hooks to create a makeshift canopy with sheer material.

### Room Rearrangements

- Just because you begin the year with the top bunk doesn't mean you have to keep that layout all year long.

- Try switching bunks, unbunking, and rearranging every so often. A new room composition can completely change the dynamics of the room.

- Don't be afraid to get creative and give new setups a trial run for a few days. If it doesn't jive, simply try something else!

29

# SHARING STUFF

## Remember when Mom taught you how to share? Put those skills to good use

Few kids grow up sharing bedrooms these days, and moving into a tiny dorm room with a total stranger can seem like a scary prospect. It's bound to be an eye-opening experience especially coming from a home where you have your own room with loads of space and the prerogative to decorate exactly as you see fit.

Strike a balance between satisfying your own whims and being respectful of your new roommate. Don't paint your walls pink, but do buy that candy-colored bedspread. Be courteous with your shared spaces, but protective of your own side of the room.

You'll be sharing more than space with this new stranger.

### Sharing the TV Set

- Your favorite show is tonight; so is your roommate's. Unfortunately they're different shows, on different channels, at the same time.

- Communicate about your respective must-see TV shows ahead of time so one of you can make alternate plans for that time.

- Try trading off week to week or checking with friends to see what they'll be tuning into.

- Many dorms have community TVs available on a first-come first-serve schedule.

### Splitting Fridge Space

- Minirefrigerators are simple to split up because of their tiny size. Each person gets a shelf, and the freezer can be divided in half.

- Slap on labels if you buy similar products to avoid any food miscommunications.

- Meticulously tagging your food might not keep a hungry roommate's hands out of it.

- If your food is disappearing before your eyes—and not into your belly—confrontation is necessary. If the "case of the missing food" persists, stick to perishables.

When the offending roommate starts clicking through the channels on your TV, nibbling on a potato chip from your bag, and freshening up with your fragrance, picture your Mom chiding you to share as a child.

Does that mean letting your roommate use your stuff, eat your food, and wear your clothes without so much as a protest? Never. But establishing rules with a level head—and allowing a little leeway with the remote control—can make living with a stranger for the next seven months much more tolerable.

## ZOOM

J. D. Salinger once said, "It's really hard to be roommates with people if your suitcases are much better than theirs." Sharing a room with someone else is really challenging, especially if you have nothing in common. Make the most of it by chalking it up as a learning experience and cocktail party chatter. You would be surprised how often "This one time in college, my roommate . . ." comes up .

## *Maintaining Boundaries*

**KEEP OUT**

- The my-wardrobe-is-your-wardrobe roommate can be spotted within the first few hours.

- He or she will peek into your shelves, compliment this shirt and those shoes, and remark that your pants would be perfect with their jacket.

- Before you know it, your roommate is walking out the door in a combination of your closet's best.

- The solution? Call him or her out on it, and stress how special your clothes are to you.

## *Lockboxes and Safes*

- Dorm rooms don't come equipped with many hiding spots for valuables, and drawers certainly don't count as secure spots.

- Little lockboxes and shoebox-size safes can keep jewelry, money, and other small treasures out of harm's way.

- Another idea is to turn your trusty dictionary into a super-secret book safe by cutting out a hollow center. It's not as if anyone actually looks words up anymore (kidding!).

# PRIVACY

## Maintaining privacy and making time for yourself in a 12 x 12 dorm room

A famous princess once said that her life was like living in a fishbowl, and sometimes living in a dorm room will feel like that. Upon entering a dorm room, it seems the only privacy you'll have for the next year is under your covers. Not so. With a little creativity you can create your own hideaway in the midst of your shared space.

Folding screens can stand in as makeshift walls to create a quiet corner. Canopies and curtains may not seem like standard dorm fare, but they make peaceful hideouts when you just need to get away.

Curtains have so much more potential than just covering windows. Canopies, just like curtains, can give you a little

### Folding Screen

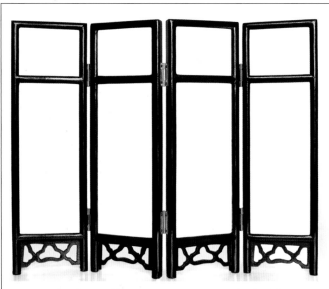

- Room dividers can be positioned by your bed, next to your desk, or near your closet to give yourself a reprieve.

- Because the screen folds up flat, simply slide it behind a door or under your bed when you don't need it around.

- You can also build your own folding screen with long plantation shutters, a few hinges, and some brightly colored paint.

- A rolling clothes rack draped with a curtain also makes a great room divider.

### Room Curtain

- Attach a few adhesive loops to the ceiling, connect with a lightweight metal rod, and slide on some bright curtains or a hemmed-up piece of fabric.

- A room curtain can be placed in front of your bed to create a little sleep cubbie.

- That corner near your closet is also an ideal spot for a drape. Craft your own dressing room for a concealed place to change clothes.

privacy right in the middle of your room. String them across the ceiling, around your bed, or in front of your closet. If nails are on the okay list at your dorm, cable systems are the simplest way to install curtains.

The way you arrange your room can have a huge impact on privacy. Try back-to-back desks, bunked beds, and curtains galore.

## Bed Canopy

- Creating a canopy is a stylish way to acquire a little privacy. There are many ways to make your own, but the gist is to suspend a long piece of fabric over your bed to create a tent-like contraption.

- If your dorm bed already has tall posts, you can simply attach sheer fabric to the four corners.

- More traditional dorm beds will require a little handiwork. With a half-dozen hooks and a sturdy pole, you'll have an enviable canopy in no time.

### Room of One's Own

- College is an unpredictable time in everyone's life, and you aren't going to have a whole lot of time to yourself.

- If you happen to deeply value alone time, a single-person dorm might be for you.

- Dorm housing is notoriously fickle, so if you find yourself stuck in a suite, bed canopies, room curtains, and folding screens help give the illusion of solitude.

# RESPECT
## Dorm unto others as they dorm unto you

They say patience is a virtue, but while living in a dorm room, patience is a necessity. Everyone has heard a tale or two of a disrespectful roommate, and by the end of the semester you'll have a story to share. No matter how sweet the first impression is, your roommate will undoubtedly disappoint you. She'll play her music too loud, or he'll keep the light on too late. But college is about getting out of your comfort zone, and no one is better at transporting you there than your roommate.

Treat your roommate the way you expect to be treated, but don't shy away from the occasional confrontation. It's much more useful to get any issues out in the open. Suppressing concerns for months on end will lead to resentment, not resolution.

### Telephone Calls

- In an age when everyone has a cell phone, making and taking calls outside of the room is not an inconvenience and it's just the considerate thing to do.

- Fielding a brief call is fine, but excuse yourself for extended chats and especially long-winded talks.

- If your roommate doesn't have the same tact, kindly suggest that he or she take the call somewhere else. If all else fails, grab your headphones.

### Headphones

- Good-quality headphones or earbuds provide instant privacy.

- If you find yourself rooming with Chatty Cathy, a brief explanation that your headphones are intended to block out any noises at all (and not just her persistent voice) will get the message across.

- Before you know it you won't even have to turn your tunes on. Simply sliding those headphones on will signal that quiet time is in effect.

Make a point to be tolerant of your roommate's imperfections. Confront the problems, not the person. Living with someone around the clock does not give you a right to criticize his or her lifestyle. Likewise, don't turn around and tell your friends tales about how "crazy" your roommate is—unless you're okay with being the topic of your roommate's conversations, too.

Take control and propose a roommate contract. This gives each of you an opportunity to discuss your needs and clearly articulate your expectations for the semester. This doesn't need to be a formal binding document; a one-on-one conversation is enough, as long as you have a deeper understanding of one another and your respective schedules, obligations, and anxieties.

## Nighttime Lights

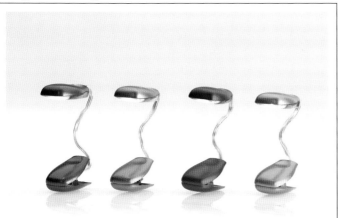

- A sleep mask won't drown out the glare of an overhead light, so kill the fluorescents after 10 p.m.

- There's no reason to use your overhead light in the first place, as bedside lamps and low-key lanterns are much more conducive to reading and studying.

- Even better is the handy clip-on book light. The little LED bulbs are appropriately bright, and the light can clip on textbooks, study notes, and laptops for late-night cramming.

### Dealing with Disrespect

- Be understanding, but don't indulge your roommate in disrespectful behavior.

- Giving up your own comfort for the sake of living in peace is just not worth your worry. If your roommate repeatedly treats you with disrespect, it's time to submit a new room request.

- If you've taken the initiative to confront problems and things haven't improved, move in with a new friend or a classmate, or simply ask for a single-person room.

# RUGS
### Cover up your dorm room's far-from-fancy floor with a stylish rug

Although some residents will strike it rich with hardwood floors, most dorms have no-frills tile flooring—you know, like the flooring of your high school hallways. It isn't fancy, but it is versatile and very convenient to cover.

Area rugs may seem ideal, but they are the priciest option, so make sure the rug you buy can be used for years. Something lightly colored will show wear after a few weeks, and regular carpet cleanings are quite an investment.

Boldly patterned rugs are the best route to go, especially if you won't have a vacuum on hand. Two accent rugs can be laid down side by side to give the illusion of wall-to-wall carpeting. Pick out rugs with your roommate, and each of you can purchase one. Not only does this help with the cost, but it also takes the guesswork out of who takes what home

## Area Rugs

- Cold tile floors are just begging to be covered up, and wall-to-wall rugs are just the remedy.

- Measure carefully and you'll soon forget that your dorm room didn't come with such soft, cushy carpeting.

- An area in the exact dimen-sions of your room might not be available, so just buy the largest you can find (and afford!).

- Another option? Consult a carpet store about cutting a piece of carpet to fit; make sure to have the edges bound for a few extra dollars!

## Accent Rugs

- Some dorm rooms are furnished with hardwood floors, which are too fancy to cover up with carpet.

- Instead, invest in a few throw rugs to keep your toes warm and your room cozy.

- Buy a few different sizes, shapes, and shades and play around with positioning them in your room. Try one in front of your bed, by your door, or under your desk chair.

- Create your own wall-to-wall runner by layering the floor with a few accent rugs.

at the end of the semester.

Because many dorm rooms are on the narrow side, a runner rug is a great cost-effective option. Like the makeshift area rug, a runner can also be created by combining two or three accent rugs.

Carpet remnants can make adequate, not to mention affordable, flooring. Save serious cash by hitting up your local carpet store and asking for leftovers.

## Runner Rugs

- Runner rugs, which are long narrow mats, will make your room look much longer than it actually is.

- If you share a room, this rug will give your room a nice division—similar to placing a piece of masking tape right down the center of the room, but infinitely more stylish.

- Make your own by stitching three or four throw rugs together, then positioning it right down the middle of your room.

## Carpet Squares

- Tour all the local carpet stores, then politely ask for leftover squares. Some will give them away for pennies, while others might offer some sort of 10 for $10 deal.

- Many brands are manufacturing carpet squares as "patchwork flooring" and charging twice the price, so look locally for places to buy.

- Similar to carpet squares is interlocking "puzzle" mats. Intended for children's playrooms, this colorful, easy-to-clean flooring will liven up even the dreariest of dorm rooms.

DECORATING

# CURTAINS

## Improve your outlook; adorn your dorm room windows with darling curtains

Whether you have a panoramic campus view or a lovely peek into your closest dining hall, curtains will make the most of your dorm room windows. If your residence hall provides miniblinds, don't ditch them, just accentuate them with interesting curtains. Colorful curtains can change the look of your whole room in a split-second.

Just as you can layer curtains with miniblinds, curtains can be doubled up as well. Try sheer shades under solid drapes. Warm sheers add a coziness, while heavier curtains keep the daylight in check. You can even try mixing and matching coordinating prints and patterns; stick with a similar color scheme to keep it from looking too tossed together.

*Sheer Curtains*

- Voile, chiffon, and other sheer textiles can bring a little romanticism to your dorm room.

- Colorful curtains will stream light in your windows in a much more tranquil way than those miniblinds, or you can just craft your own.

- Simply go to the fabric store and buy a few yards of sheer fabric. Hem the edges an inch or two, then slide the fabric on a rod.

- Even easier is draping fabric along the top of your window using adhesive hooks. Voila! Instant valance.

*Roman Shades*

- A sleek roman shade—a flat, compact window covering—provides a classic decoration while sleekly covering your window.

- Roman shades hang from the window casing for a neat, streamlined style

- The traditional Roman

shade features a flat panel, but fancier styles tout overlapping folds and intricate textures.

- They come in countless colors, but don't spend big bucks on a decorated shade. Because the surface is so smooth, they can be embellished with ease.

## MAKE IT EASY

Curtains can be made from scratch in a matter of minutes, even if you don't have any experience with a sewing machine. A large piece of fabric or an extra flat sheet can be turned into delightful window coverings with just a few straight stitches.

## Blackout Curtains

- Nothing promises a good night's sleep like a blackout curtain . . . and nothing promises an abundance of missed early morning classes.

- These thick curtains block out sunlight in its entirety, making 11 a.m. appear to be 11 p.m.

- These curtains are incredibly efficient for catching a mid-afternoon nap, and they're also handy when the weekend rolls around.

- Only purchase these if you can deal with round-the-clock darkness, because you'll never be awakened by sunlight again.

## Miniblinds

- Miniblinds aren't aesthetically remarkable, but they sure are reliable.

- If your dorm room isn't outfitted with miniblinds, they aren't worth the investment for only a year of use.

- Instead, buy a few bundles of inch-wide ribbon. Measure your window top to bottom, then cut strands of ribbon in the same length. Hem the edge an inch or two thick. Finally, slide the ribbons on a curtain rod side by side to create an equally airy window covering.

DECORATING

# POSTERS

## Deck the walls with posters that drip with personality

When it comes to dorm room walls, many universities prohibit painting, but that doesn't mean you have to live with and love the plain white walls. From movie posters to band paraphernalia to art prints, posters add personality to otherwise ho-hum walls.

Your parents complained every time you added another poster to your ever-expanding collection at home, and now there'll be no one around to protest placing a Rolling Stones record cover next to your *Superbad* movie poster.

That doesn't mean you need to cover every inch of your ho-hum white walls with your pop culture favorites just because you can, but posters bring a lot of personality for very little money.

If there is a time that it's socially acceptable to wallpaper

### *Music Posters*

- Show off your complex taste in music with a mishmash of band posters. Picture the Rolling Stones alongside Death Cab for Cutie, or Prince next to Lil Wayne.

- Create your own music poster by collaging different album covers collected from antiques stores and tag sales. Vintage records have a classic old-school vibe.

- If your taste in music is as fickle as your latest favorite song, the music posters can be swapped as often as your iPod playlists.

### *Movie Posters*

- Covering your walls with posters of your favorite movies is an easy way to attract like-minded friends.

- Hang *Breakfast at Tiffany's* alongside *Annie Hall* to show your love for the Big Apple, or *The Godfather* next to *The Graduate* to confirm your adoration of old films.

- ebay is a gold mine for antique film posters, and because they're a dime a dozen, they can be purchased for pocket change.

- Also hit up local movie theaters to snag free posters of more recent flicks.

your walls with posters, it's college. White walls aren't exactly the most inspiring things to stare at for hours on end, so surround yourself with something that stimulates you while you study—or procrastinate.

## CD Pocket Posters

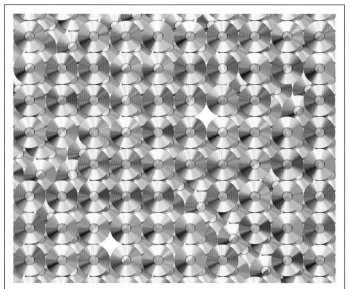

- A cool pocket poster turns compact discs into wall-worthy art. Use this poster to stash your favorite DVDs, or utilize that stack of long-forgotten music disks.

- You can also make your own CD poster by adhering rows of clear pocket flaps to the wall in a rectangular shape.

- The key is to slide your CDs in with the labels facing the wall, creating an awesome holographic effect. When the sun hits it just right, you'll have daylight dancing around your room.

## Artwork

- Bring a little highbrow culture into your run-of-the-mill room with prints of paintings and artsy photographs.

- Artists like Picasso and Monet are particularly dorm friendly because of their bright colors and recognizable characteristics.

- Support community artists with their creative endeavors; not only will their pieces bring a bit of local color to your room, but they're far more affordable—and authentic—than classic art prints.

DECORATING

# MIRRORS

## A little reflection makes small rooms seem larger, enhances natural light, and adds depth to the decor

Mirrors are one of the single best-kept secrets among interior decorators. They add the illusion of space and heaps of style—and they're useful to boot.

A full-length mirror is a must. Maybe you don't need to check your head-to-toe reflection before heading to a lecture, but for job interviews, class presentations, and first dates, an

up-and-down once-over will save you from potential humiliation, like realizing your tie is ten inches too short or noticing your socks are fully visible . . . and mismatched.

You don't even need to worry about mounting it on the wall; leaning a frameless mirror against the wall will extend the line of the room and open up the area. With a little

### Full-Length Mirrors

- Fastening a full-length mirror to the back of your dorm room door is the ideal height to get the full head-to-toe glance. Use S hooks to mount it without nails.

- A full-length mirror looks even more stylish artfully propped up against the wall (and so will your reflection). "Anchor" it with a stack of vintage books or a doorstop.

- Freestanding mirrors conveniently rotate. Adjust the angle to fully catch the light to brighten up your entire room.

### Cosmetic Mirrors

- You could lug your makeup to the bathroom to do your primping in the fluorescent light every morning.

- Or you could invest in a nice vanity mirror to keep atop your desk for early morning makeup and impromptu touch-ups.

- Look for a vanity mirror equipped with an LED light. This natural-looking light is optimal for makeup and will be a much better option than that overhead fixture of yours.

handyman prowess, two or three mirrors can be hinged together to create a reflective folding screen.

Hang mirrors on the wall anywhere you have additional wall space: above your closet, next to your desk, by your door. If possible hang mirrors on opposite walls—but not directly across from each other—so they can reflect sunlight and brighten up the room.

Laying a mirror flat on your desk shelf can create a lovely vignette when topped with perfume bottles and pretty jars filled with jewelry.

## Decorative Mirrors

- Mirrors make your itty-bitty room look twice its size—no small feat.

- Mirrors with fun trims and ornate frames can add some much-needed style to your wall space.

- Decorative mirrors are cut into cute shapes like circles, hearts, and flowers and are self-adhesive to attach straight onto the wall.

- Try bunching classic square mirrors or attaching a handful of small ones to create a larger wall mirror with interesting "broken" patterns.

### Keeping Mirrors Clean

- When your walls are covered in mirrors, keeping them clean is of the utmost importance.

- A bottle of glass cleaner and a roll of paper towels should be perpetually handy.

- Make it a point to thoroughly wipe them down weekly. It takes two seconds, but makes all the difference.

- Mirrors make dusty surfaces that much more noticeable, so keep those clean, too.

DECORATING

43

# DECALS

## When wallpaper is off-limits, wall decals decorate with spunk

Wall decals are the new kid in school when it comes to room decor. The inspired stickers attach to any type of surface and can be rearranged as often as your class schedule.

Did your room's last resident leave an unsightly stamp on the wall? Slap on a flashy decal, and you'll have the coolest room around. Do the all-white walls wear you out? Channel your inner child and polka dot your room.

The appeal of decals is that you can change your walls as often as you change your underwear. Or, um, maybe that isn't the best analogy for a college freshman.

The point is, press them on wherever you wish, then peel them off when you're ready for something new. Wall decals can take on the look of wallpaper, or they can simply add a hint of whimsy to your room. Because your world will revolve

### Chalkboard Decals

### Wall Decals

- Channel your grade school roots with an authentically adorable chalkboard.

- Apply to your wall and you can write and erase to your heart's content.

- Be cautious where you slap on this decal. If you put it over your bed or above your desk, you or your belongings will be covered in chalk dust.

- Close to your study spot is ideal, as this chalkboard will come in handy for math problems—if only you were still doing simple addition.

- Many decals go past simple wall decor and end up taking on the illusion of professional wallpaper.

- Floor-to-ceiling polka dots or stripes do such a convincing job that your residence hall director might accuse you of breaking rules.

- All-over polka dots or stripes are stylish but tedious; a few well-placed decals make just as big an impression and require far less work.

44

around your bed, consider using the space above where you sleep, study, and socialize as your canvas. From trompe l'oeil headboards to quirky chandeliers to press-on picture frames, you can create an oasis in your space.

Remember when you used to collect cute stickers as a kid? Think of your wall as your sticker book and decorate away.

## Frame Decals

- Frame decals make it possible to stick photos right on the wall.

- Because they're removable *and* reusable, you can swap out the pictures as you please.

- A fancy rococo style of frame looks delightfully kitschy on dorm room walls—it's a beautifully fancy wall decor in a pleasingly minimal dorm room.

- If you want something even more creative than full-blown frames, photo-corner adhesives are bright and playful.

## Novelty Decals

- From footballs to flower blossoms, from polka dots to pets, novelty wall decals are a quick way to introduce personality.

- Remember that less is more. When it comes to wall stickers, give considerable thought to where you slap them on.

- To create a look that's fanciful but not overdone, limit yourself to two or three wall stickers at a time.

- Don't go too cutesy. Flowers, polka dots, and zoo animals are a little too much for college kids.

DECORATING

# GREENERY

## Breathe new life into a dorm room with plants, flowers, and other ecofriendly greenery

The easiest way to add life to your room? Get a pet. But since pets are outlawed in residence halls, lively green plants are the next best thing.

Plants are a bright green breath of fresh air, and more than just looking nice, they have an immeasurable effect on well-being. Plants have been proven to improve concentration and strengthen mental health—both crucial qualities for a productive college student.

Small potted plants are perfect for your desk top, while tall plants can fill in an otherwise empty corner.

Flowers are a fab addition, but keeping fresh ones around will add up. Save floral purchases for special occasions (like

### Bright Plants

- Look for plants that have a long shelf life and live without arduous watering.

- Hanging baskets are a great way to incorporate plants without taking up any valuable surface space; dangle them from a removable plant hook placed on a door.

- Ivy, cacti, and spider plants are low maintenance and high impact. Aloe vera is another easy plant to have around, and the medicating extract will be nice to have on hand.

### Fresh Flowers

- Carnations, lilies, and sunflowers last up to two weeks and bring a serious shot of color to any room.

- Cut off the bottoms of the stems as soon as you get fresh flowers home, then put them directly in water.

- Put a spoonful of sugar in the vase to "feed" your flowers, and top them off with fresh water every few days.

- Instead of using classic—and cliché—vases, try something unexpected, like a vintage milk jar, old-school soda bottle, or quirky mug.

parents weekend). Instead of a momentary bouquet, treat yourself to gorgeous silk buds. Fancy faux flowers are nearly as elegant as the real thing, and having any sort of flower around the room will add an instant air of sophistication.

The right plant will add fragrance *and* color to your small room without taking up much space or requiring too much attention. Unless you go with artificial greenery, you'll have to remember to water every few days. If you can get a routine down—water after your morning coffee or before you crawl into bed—your plants will thrive effortlessly.

## Faux Flowers

- Faux flowers are a great alternative to fresh ones, but make sure you accentuate their kitschiness by buying only the brightest and funkiest of blossoms and displaying them in unique, playful vases.

- Artificial blossoms have gotten a bad reputation, so know what to look for. Stick with silk flowers, sparse arrangements, and nice vases.

- Make your own decorative pillows by covering cushions with silk blooms. A needle and thread will work flawlessly, while a hot glue gun is a smart shortcut.

## Fish Tanks

- Fish tanks aren't greenery, per se, but they sure bring a lot of life to a dorm room.

- Only buy fish that have long shelf lives. There's nothing worse than a fish that goes belly up after a few hours without food.

- When it comes to fish tanks, the simpler, the better. Classic fish bowls are time-tested, and you can always add a few aquarium plants to bring a nice touch of bright green.

DECORATING

# VERTICAL SPACE
## When storage is lacking, make the most of your space by looking up

When you're sharing a room the size of a closet, making the most of every inch of space is a must. Think of your room as New York City; it would just be silly to build a one-story building in the middle of the Big Apple. Take a cue from Manhattan and use those untapped resources to build up.

Maximize your vertical space with tall shelves, compact furniture, and stacks and stacks *and stacks* of bins, buckets, even books. Think with creativity and look for surface area where you least expect it. Reconfigure milk crates into colorful cubbyholes. Turn a stack of old science textbooks or ages-old fashion magazines into a grand side table.

Few dorms allow residents to hammer holes, so traditional wall shelving is out of the question. Instead, think of the possibilities of floor shelves, desk shelves, even ladder shelves.

### Shelving

- Not being able to use screws and pins in your walls limits your shelving capabilities, but that doesn't mean you have to lead a surface-less existence.

- A bookshelf that's tall and thin can squeeze in between furniture and occupy any empty floor space you can find.

- Look for CD and DVD cabinets to store small knickknacks.

- Look for shallow bookshelves in a wood stain that matches your dorm furniture to rest on top of your desk or dresser—or both!

### Compact Furniture

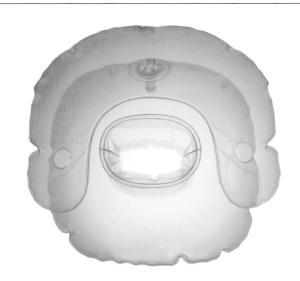

- Compact furniture that can be stashed under a bed or inside a closet will be invaluable for unexpected in-room get-togethers.

- Outdoor supply stores are gold mines for fold-up furniture. With the right decorative pillow, a lawn chair becomes a cool, comfy seat.

- Another great option is investing in a few director's chairs, which are stylish, inexpensive, and surprisingly cozy.

Fold-up furniture—from chairs to tables to laptop stands—can be artfully arranged on adhesive hooks when not in use. The very same hooks can turn your baseball glove stockpile or vintage jewelry collection into bona fide wall art (and what a convenient way to stay organized, too).

## Stackable Bins

- Stackable storage—anything from milk crates to nesting bins to snap-lid containers— can be stacked to the ceiling if need be.

- Milk crates cannot only cart your stuff during the move, but they can make a really cool storage shelf. Simply stack them with openings facing forward, creating colorful little cubbies.

- "Nesting" bins are equally good at multitasking, in that they can stow your stuff while you're transporting from dorm to home and are stylish enough to use as decorative storage.

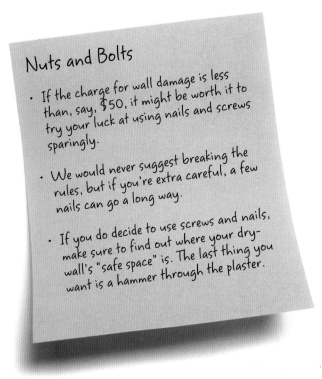

### Nuts and Bolts

- If the charge for wall damage is less than, say, $50, it might be worth it to try your luck at using nails and screws sparingly.

- We would never suggest breaking the rules, but if you're extra careful, a few nails can go a long way.

- If you do decide to use screws and nails, make sure to find out where your drywall's "safe space" is. The last thing you want is a hammer through the plaster.

FURNISHING

49

# COUCH
## Give your bed a rest and chill out on a cozy couch

Despite daydreams of decorating your room with cool lounge chairs and sectional sofas, there's no way around it: Your bed will be the largest piece of furniture in your dorm room.

Because dorms are so compact, it's likely that your bed will moonlight as a couch. Instead of cringing every time a friend plops his stinky feet on your comforter, keep a few blankets and pillows handy to throw down when pals drop in.

If you're lucky enough to squeeze an actual sofa in your room, stick to a convenient love-seat size. Children's departments in home decor stores often carry couches that are low to the ground and smaller in size, but still big enough to fit a few college bodies.

Convertible seating is another smart option, specifically

### Do-It-Yourself Daybeds

- With enough throw pillows and a few extra blankets, your dorm bed can transition from sleep to play.

- The key to turning your dorm bed into a daybed is to line up large-sized pillows along the wall as a stand-in headboard. European pillows are perfect for this.

- Create a focal point with a contrasting pillowcase, decorative pillow, or favorite stuffed animal.

- Go ahead and hide your own bedtime pillow—unless you don't mind friends sitting on the pillow *you* sleep on.

### Loft Beds

- If you can conceal an entire couch under your bed, consider yourself lucky. And consider your dorm too cool for school.

- The elevated bed will be the ideal place for sleeping, slowing down, and quietly studying, while your couch can be the touchstone for entertaining.

- Any couch will do. If you have the space but you don't have cash to spare, a fitted sheet can transform a Salvation Army sofa in seconds.

in loftable dorm rooms. Futons can transition from bed to couch and loungers. Before you buy, carefully measure the unbound space in your room. Although futons can transition from bed to couch, they aren't completely stashable.

If you really don't have the space to spare, you can also find beanbag sectionals that can be stashed underneath a bed and inflatable couches that can be blown up at a moment's notice. Pass on pricey slipcovers and simply use a fitted sheet or pin on a large piece of fabric.

## Futons

- A futon will last long after your college years end. Invest in a sturdy frame, and the futon pad and pillows can be swapped out every few seasons or simply recovered to refresh the appearance.

- Don't splurge for fancy futon covers. Fitted sheets are the perfect size.

- Futons are essentially minimal sleeper sofas, so consider this a warning: If friends catch on that you have an extra sleeping space, your room will be adopted as the go-to room for all-night movie marathons.

## Loungers

- A lounger is a cross between a futon and a floor pillow. Nestled directly on the ground, it can flip up into a chair or lay flat like a bed.

- Many have adjustable settings, allowing you to recline as much or as little as you want.

- A lounger doubles as a snug sleeping cot. It's far more comfortable than a sleeping bag and much less of a hassle than an inflatable mattress.

FURNISHING

# COZY SEATING

Because your bed can only seat so many, space-conscious dorm-friendly seats are essential

Dorm-room seating should be as comfortable as it is compact, as aesthetically pleasing as it is pal friendly. With a few cozy seats on hand, you can create a dorm lounge right in your room at the drop of a . . . beanbag.

Most cozy chairs can be stashed away if need be. Disk and butterfly chairs fold up with ease, and beanbags can be crammed into the back of your closet.

Floor pillows and lounge cushions are perhaps the best multitaskers of all, because they can be tossed on top of your bed to make a snug study nest or scattered around the floor for an impromptu hangout.

The goal is to find a favorite study spot away from the

## Armchairs

- If you don't have room to accommodate a couch but can spare a few feet of floor space, an overstuffed armchair is the next best thing.

- If Mom and Dad have a cast-off armchair from the 1970s, grab a slipcover or pay a few hundred dollars to get it reupholstered.

- When it comes to armchairs, don't skip over the children's departments for pint-size seating. They're considerably smaller than their full-size counterparts, but they'll suit a college student just fine.

## Collapsible Chairs

- The butterfly chair, inspired by the original B.K.F. Chair by architect Jorge Ferrari Hardoy, has been a mainstay in dorm rooms since the 1980s.

- Disk chairs are comfortable and cute, and they can be squeezed into even the

smallest dorm room. The sleek circle shape is perfect for a decorative pillow.

- These chairs are cozy and collapsible, but they don't offer much in the way of neck and back support when it comes to studying.

confines of your bed and desk chair. It just isn't healthy to spend too much time atop your bed when you're not sleeping, and you'll get restless spending hours on end boxed in your desk.

Comfy spur-of-the-moment seats are just the answer. Make sure to access all your options. Design companies are expanding their seat selections by the season. You can find beanbag chairs in the shape of disks, rockers, and even armchairs.

## *Beanbags*

- When beanbags first hit the home-goods scene, they came in T-shirt–soft cotton that busted at the seams within weeks. These days you can find the whimsical seat in sturdy denim and brushed twill or luxurious fur and animal print.

- If you (or your room-mate) are accident-prone, stick with removable and machine-washable slipcovers.

- A similar option is the Fatboy, a branded bean-bag alternative that has a unique rectangular shape that allows you to nestle in it like you do a lounge chair.

## *Floor Pillows*

- Scattered around the room, overstuffed floor pillows can create a cozy space wherever they end up.

- Cylinder- and cube-shaped cushions can be scattered and stacked to create a makeshift lounge.

- Sometimes sleek floor pillows can be hard to find, so take a peek in the pet department. As far-fetched as it sounds, stylish dog beds are phenomenal for dorm floor lounging.

FURNISHING

# LIGHTING

## Forgo fluorescents; embrace lamps, lanterns, and string lights

The only thing less welcoming than a room with fluorescent lighting is a dorm room with fluorescent lighting. Use the overhead light as sparingly as possible, and lighten up your surroundings with cheery desk lamps, soft lanterns, and festive holiday lights.

Since a desktop lamp will take up some of your treasured surface space and an electrical outlet, look for a lamp that has a few built-in outlets in its base. High-tech lights undoubtedly look cool, but classic lamps are very customizable. They often come with mix-and-match options: a variety of bases and shades that can be switched out when you get tired of your current one. Lamp shades are incredibly conducive to adding your own crafty touch. You can paint the base and swap the shade. Cheap shades can be spray painted, recovered,

### Floor Lamps

- Forget the overhead light. Seriously, forget it's even there. A few well-placed floor lamps around the room can brighten up your space in a delightful way.

- Three-way lightbulbs are key. They allow you to

  adjust just how bright you want your room.

- Be mindful of wattage restrictions, however.

- Look for floor lamps that have a narrow footprint to maximize your floor space.

### Task Lamps

- A task lamp is just a fancy term for a lamp that sheds light on an activity like reading, study, or playing video games (hey, a college student has to unwind sometime!).

- Many task lamps include high-tech features like built-in speakers, outlets, and electrical chargers.

- If you aren't into the industrial style of a task lamp, a classic table lamp is just as useful and even more stylish.

and embellished to fit your taste.

With a little bit of clever wiring, you can hang lanterns and chandeliers from your ceiling.

If you don't have the budget to buy a variety of lamps, invest in one floor lamp and simply swap out the bulbs of your ceiling fixture.

## *Lantern Lighting*

- Paper lanterns come in bright colors and patterns and really lighten up an entire room.

- Hanging a few in the corner will draw the eye upward, making the ceiling seem impossibly higher than the humble eight feet.

- The paper pendant lights are so lightweight they can be easily strung up with a few adhesive hooks.

- Paper lanterns look even better in groups of twos or threes or in a handful of different colors.

## *String Lights*

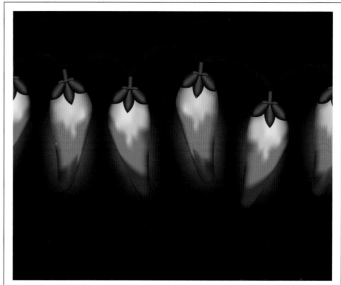

- Festive string lights add a fantastic glow year-round. Attach them *anywhere*— from your bed to your window to your desk—with tiny adhesive eye hooks.

- Rope lights are essentially just enclosed Christmas lights; they're a little less holiday-centric and even more conducive to year-round lighting.

- Miniature lantern lights are a more sophisticated way to bring color through string lights without suspending strands of pineapples and palm trees.

FURNISHING

# INVESTMENTS
## If you shop smartly, buying nice things now can pay off in the future

Your early twenties are an ideal time to take a close look at your belongings and consider the long-term value of things. By the time you enter college, you will have most likely accumulated a few possessions that make you proud.

Perhaps you acquired an antique saucer from a great aunt, or your grandfather passed down his vintage golf clubs. Maybe you treated yourself to a fancy silk scarf, or you bought mugs

from the memorable places you visited. Some collections, no matter how miniature they may seem, will accrue value over the years. The exception? Skip the Beanies Babies and opt for something you can actually use.

When you purchase new items for your room, no matter how small in size or price, put a lot of thought into how long you can use these things.

### Antique Knickknacks

- Little knickknacks, like teacups, saucers, and sugar bowls, are pretty catchalls to set on your dresser, atop your desk, or in your drawers.

- One adorable mug can keep your keys in place, while another can hold your

pocket change. A petite plate can catch day-to-day jewelry.

- Comb through tag sales, antiques auctions, and vintage stores. But first ask Grandma if she has any knickknacks to spare.

### Hand-Me-Downs

- Fancy hand-me-down vases, pitchers, and other dishware can be impossibly glamorous in a dorm room.

- Serving trays and cake trays, especially in silver and sterling, will upgrade the surface of a dorm dresser or desk in an instant.

- Make sure nothing's too valuable, and ask your parent's permission before snagging anything.

- At the same time, don't be afraid of antiques. It isn't useful if it's too "precious" to use.

Repurpose knickknacks you might never have given a glance: Doilies become frameable art, ashtrays store necklaces and earrings, and tea canisters stow odds and ends in style.

It's like putting money into the stock market: The up-front cost is nerve-racking, but the long-term returns are well worth it. An old-fashioned steamer trunk might cost more than a few plastic storage tubs, but the trunk will stick with you through your first dorm, first apartment, and first house.

## Global Accessories

- Globes instantly heighten a room's global style. If you don't have space for a full-size globe, scatter a group of three mini-orbs as a shelf vignette. Suspend a globe from the ceiling with fishing line and a small hook.

- Consider using an oversize map as wall decor. Simply unfold a traveler's map, iron it on a low setting, and attach it to the wall with easy-to-remove adhesives.

- Old posters with international and astrological themes intended for grade school classrooms can also make unique wall art.

## Antique Tapestries

- Elegant heirloom room decor can take your room from mundane dorm to exceptional apartment.

- Oriental rugs and tapestries cover up a tired tile floor or attach to the wall to hide plain white walls.

- Replica Oriental rugs can be found for reasonable prices at home stores and look phenomenal juxtaposed with the modern interior of a dorm.

- ebay is a gold mine for would-be heirlooms like rugs, tapestries, and Oriental textiles.

FURNISHING

# STORAGE SPACE

## Make the most of your small space and store your belongings in style

Storage is hard to come by in a compact dorm room, but that doesn't mean you have to cramp your lifestyle. You can continue living large—just in a more organized manner. Leave no surface uncovered, leave no drawer unturned. Even unassuming corners of the room and cracks between furniture can turn into unanticipated storage spaces.

Cardboard boxes are fine to use while moving into and away from the dorm, but don't live out of them all semester. Invest in more sophisticated storage *now* and you'll use it for years to come. A steamer trunk, often uncovered in dusty antiques stores, can conceal anything from clothes to textbooks and can be nice enough to serve as a coffee table.

### Under-the-Bed Containers

- Stackable, sliding storage chests can stow your winter clothes, extra school supplies, and other items you don't need on a frequent basis.

- Because these containers are typically half the width of a bed, stack two or three and push them against the wall.

- With at least half of the under-bed area unclaimed, you can conveniently store everyday essentials in easy to access drawers and crates.

### Stacked Tubs

- Colorful plastic tubs are perfect for storing blankets and pillows.

- Tubs take up space, so it's best to store them in the back of your bed and stuff them with things you don't need on a daily basis.

- Plastic-bag makers are now manufacturing tubs out of a lightweight plastic. Although they're less sturdy than stronger plastic containers, a major plus is that they're completely collapsible.

Plastic tubs and drawers aren't particularly stylish, but they're cheap and useful and can be covered with contact paper or coated with plastic-friendly spray paint. Wire cube-shaped shelves, often found in home-supply stores, are stackable and incredibly useful. The texture resembles a sturdy chicken wire, which allows you to hang totes, clothes, and accessories with S hooks directly on the shelving.

## Plastic Drawers

- Available in a variety of sizes, plastic drawers are incredibly functional.

- Larger drawers can hold closet necessities like socks and T-shirts or perishable food like cereal and chips (you know, the essentials).

- Desktop drawers, about the size of a crayon box, are the ideal size to stash study supplies.

- They also make an unassuming and incredibly well-situated jewelry box.

## Shipping Stuff

- If you overpack, send stuff home that you have no use for instead of keeping it around and allowing it to use up valuable space.

- You won't need a winter coat in August, so hold off on season-specific things until they're absolutely necessary.

- It's truly better to underestimate what you'll need. Not only does it save space, but it'll be a wonderful excuse to get a lovely care package from your parents or to hightail it to the mall.

FURNISHING

# SHEETS

## Have a good night's sleep on an ancient mattress with the addition of great sheets

After spending years sleeping on the same bed, comfortable sheets can make a new bed instantly cozier. Selecting your sheets seems nearly as complicated as planning your class schedule. There are so many things to consider, like thread count, fabric, color, and fit. Search for sheets similar in feel to those you use at home.

Colleges emphasize the importance of extra-long sheets, and while these are certainly something to look into, they are not a necessity. Bedding for the average twin-size bed will certainly fit a dorm mattress, but a few too many trips to the laundromat can result in seriously shrunken sheets. There's nothing more aggravating than linens that don't stay

### Colorful Sheets

- Whatever you do, don't buy white sheets. Sure, they look lovely in fancy hotel rooms and straight out of the package.

- After a few nights of you going to bed covered in campus grime (you can say "ewww!" now, but just wait), those white sheets will be

less than pristine.

- Since your bed doubles as a couch for friends *and* a study spot for you, snack stains and coffee spills will inevitably appear.

- The brighter or darker the sheets, the easier time you'll have hiding stains.

### Mix-and-Match Patterns

- If there is ever a time to sleep in striped sheets, under a floral comforter, atop a polka-dot pillow, it's college.

- Because the room itself is so understated, you have the prerogative to go above

and beyond with your bedding.

- When it comes to mixing and matching, stick with a similar color palate or look for patterns that are comparable in size, like itty-bitty polka dots with thin stripes.

secure—especially on a ten-year-old vinyl mattress. Suffice it to say, extra-long sheets might be worth the extra money, but only if your university suggests it.

The selection of twin-size sheets are infinitely more interesting than that of extra-long sheets, so if you have your heart set on a certain set of twin-size bedding, buy a few and gently wash and dry them on a delicate setting.

The higher the thread count, the softer the sheet, but there's no reason to spend $500 for 1,000-thread-count sheets. Triple-digit thread counts are more than nice enough.

## Multiple Sheet Sets

- Invest in several sets of sheets. Buy a few of the same color, or switch it up and buy contrasting shades, which will change the whole look of your dorm room each time you swap your sheets.

- No matter how organized you are, you probably won't be doing your laundry on a biweekly basis.

- Instead of running to the laundromat just to wash your sheets, keep a clean set around at all times and remember to change them every ten days.

### Linen Service

- Many dorms offer optional weekly or biweekly linen services. Much like a hotel, a linen service will arrange to have your room stocked with bath towels and bed linens upon arrival.

- Although the convenience is hard to beat, it's really not worth the financial commitment. You're going to be washing your clothes, so you might as well wash your sheets, too.

- If you really question your ability to wash your sheets and towels with any regularity, a linen service might be worth it.

# BLANKETS
## Ease dorm-room drafts and add depth to decor

Dorm temperatures are impossible to predict, regardless of seasons. Sometimes air-conditioners work *too* well, other times they scarcely even circulate the air. Sometimes heating units are impossibly toasty, other times they have ice cycles dangling from their depths.

Even though extra room is lacking, you really can't have too many blankets. They're a breeze to store; simply hang them up in your closet alongside your clothes or tuck them in your dresser drawers (they make the perfect padding for your delicates).

If you want to keep one on your bed for easy access, fold it crosswise and lay it crosswise on the edge of your bed. This adds texture and depth to your bedspread and gives you an opportunity to add even more color to your room.

### Throws

- Keep a few contrasting-color throw blankets on hand to add style and warmth to your room.

- Draping one over your desk chair will transform an ordinary piece of dorm furniture into something a little more exceptional. A cozy blanket will transform a rickety wood chair into a comfy reading spot.

- A small throw also makes a great slipcover or tablecloth if you're in a dorm decor pinch.

### Down Blankets

- A down blanket's breathable insulation keeps you warm in the winter and not too toasty in the summer.

- Down is lightweight and extremely compressible. It can be folded up and stored in spaces half the size fleece or flannel can.

- Down blankets are designed to go *under* a comforter—the middle layer between bedspread and sheets—so they're cut smaller than typical twin sizes.

- If you have allergies, cover your down blanket with an allergy-proof dust mite encasing.

A few grab-and-go blankets are great to have for outings to football games or adventures to the park. Buy blankets in a variety of sizes so that you have a nice selection and don't have to do laundry every time you (and your blanket) have an outdoor excursion or picnic.

## Flannel Coverlets

- Whether you listen to garage rock and shower once a week or not, flannel is a staple for college students.

- The lightweight woven wool fabric adds a layer of warmth without making you overheat. And the hip collegiate pattern certainly boosts this blanket's cool.

- Similar to a fleece blanket, you can make your own flannel throw by fringing two sheets of the plaid fabric, then tying the trimming together.

## Knit Afghans

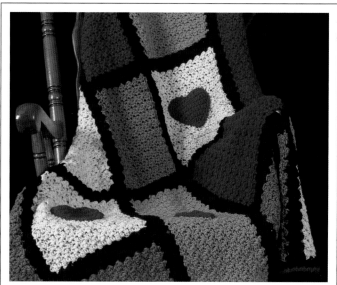

- Knitting isn't the pastime it once was, but chances are that someone you love has knitted a blanket for you at some point in your life.

- If you own any special knitted blankets or afghans, bring them along for the usability *and* sentimentality.

- Don't have any afghans around the house? They're a dime a dozen on eBay and don't cost more than that either.

# BEDSPREAD
## The comforter sets the stage for your entire dorm room's decor

Since you'll be living with plain white walls, you can literally choose any color your heart desires—with the exception of white, which will prove impossible to keep clean after just a few days in the dorm.

Patterns don't show wear and tear, and they'll expertly conceal those inevitable coffee spills. Even better is a double-sided bedspread that reverses to reveal a contrasting color or print. Flipping the bedspread will give your dorm room a whole new look. Another plus? A reversible comforter enables you to wash your bedding half as often (not that you need the enabling).

Decorative comforters don't have removable covers, which means they're more than likely not machine washable (to be sure, always check the label). Duvet covers, on the other hand,

### *Duvets*

- What sets duvets apart from any other bedspread is that they typically come in two separate entities—a duvet cover (the pretty top layer) and a duvet insert (essentially a plain comforter filled with down or a down alternative).

- Duvets are convenient for dorm dwellers because the cover can be easily removed and tossed in a washing machine, whereas comforters often require dry cleaning.

- A good duvet insert can last years, so you can swap different duvet covers if your style changes.

### *Quilts*

- The great thing about quilts is that in addition to looking refined, they always have some sort of personal significance. They're special for reasons beyond style.

- Another plus? They're fantastically cozy and bring a decidedly country look to the room.

- Even if your quilt wasn't hand sewn by your great-grandmother and even if it was, in fact, picked up at the corner thrift store, quilts seem to carry—and create—history wherever they end up.

can be easily removed and tossed in the washer. Because they're so cozy and convenient, duvets can be used in place of a comforter, blanket, and top sheet, which completely removes the effort of making your bed in the morning.

Another option? If you have an old comforter that's no longer quite your style but is still in good shape, simply buy a new duvet cover for it.

## MAKE IT EASY

Cool duvet covers are hard to find—and expensive to boot. Make your own by purchasing two extra flat sheets the same size as your duvet insert and lay them with their decorative sides together. Sew around the edges, leaving a full edge unfinished. Turn the cover right side out and slip in your duvet insert. To finish the edge, stitch on small snaps.

## Bright Bedspreads

- Like your dorm room sheets, opt for the most colorful pattern you can find when it comes to dorm bedding.

- A light-colored comforter just isn't the brightest idea (pun intended), because it'll be so hard to keep clean.

- If you have your heart set on an understated comforter, opt for a white machine-washable variety and keep the bleach bottle handy.

- If bright colors don't suit your style, opt for solid navy or charcoal gray and colorful accent pillows and a nice patterned blanket.

### Make Your Bed

- A well-made bed makes all the difference in the overall aesthetics of your dorm room.

- Taking two seconds to smooth out your sheets guarantees a cleaner-looking room and even sweeter dreams.

- Make a habit of making your bed the second you hop out. This eliminates procrastination and enhances your room.

- If you still need a motivator to straighten your sheets, making your bed will make taking a nap that much easier.

# PILLOWS

Make your room fashionable *and* comfortable with an abundance
of pillows

An abundance of pillows can transform your bed into a fabulous provisional couch. Color coordination is key. Buy a handful of different sizes in a similar pattern, or buy different-colored pillows in a similar palate and size.

Don't be too overzealous with the decorative pillow. If you load your bed in excess of eight, you'll spend more time rearranging your bed decor than you'll spend studying. Odd numbers are always stylistically better, but balance is key. Create an unexpected asymmetry with three to five pillows.

You'll want a variety of sizes for optimal comfort. Oversize pillows can be tossed on the floor for spontaneous lounging, and overstuffed poufs can stand in as an extra seat.

### Bedtime Pillows

- When you go pillow shopping, consider what kind of sleeper you are: Side sleepers should stick with firm, and stomach sleepers should go with soft.

- Synthetic pillows are inexpensive, but only last a few years. A natural-fill pillow is a bit pricier, but can last up to ten years.

- A pillow protector is a great idea to lengthen the life of your pillow. Laundering your pillows in the washing machine is also a must.

### Decorative Pillows

- A variety of colors, patterns, and sizes will spice up your bed top, regardless of how cool or classic your comforter is.

- Choose one consistency—perhaps a color scheme or a similar print—to bring a little control to your room's decor chaos.

- Armed with a needle and thread, you can sew your own decorative pillows with T-shirts, scarves, and mismatched fabric remnants.

Many pillows may be dry clean only, but seek out ones that are machine washable for convenience. Check the tag for directions before you rip it off your pillow. The most important factor is that they dry completely. Any dampness left in a pillow will cause mold to form. If your pillow is fluffy without clumps, it's dry.

Another option both for sleeping and bed decoration is the European square pillow, a 26-inch square-shaped pillow. Because of its unique shape and firmness, this pillow can stand in as a headboard tucked behind your decorative pillows.

## MAKE IT EASY

The simplest way to transform your dorm bed into a bona fide daybed is to add a headboard lengthwise. Anything can stand in for a traditional headboard: Try stretched colored canvas, fabric-covered foam, or wall murals. The easiest way to make your own headboard is to buy a few large pieces of corkboard the length of your bed and twice the height. .

### *Body Pillows*

- Body pillows, as well as more decorative bolster pillows, conform to your body and provide added support for sleeping and lounging.

- If you aren't used to sleeping in a narrow bed, body pillows are a great buffer between the wall and you, the restless sleeper.

- Because of their elongated length, body pillows are a crucial component for transforming your bed into a daytime couch.

### *Study Pillows*

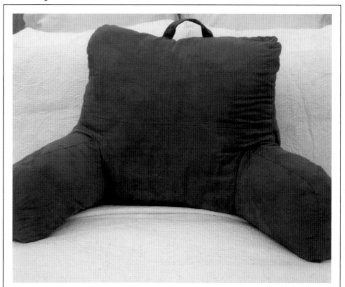

- An armchair pillow, widely known as the boyfriend pillow, makes a fantastic study buddy—regardless of the feminine name,

- They offer ideal support for studying in your bed, on the floor, or in a chair without arm rests.

- Prop a boyfriend pillow at the head of your bed and suddenly you have your own little recliner—or the closest to a recliner armchair you'll have this year, anyway.

# MATTRESS COVER

## Make sleeping on an old-as-you-are mattress endurable—and surprisingly comfortable

Mattress toppers are a must if you hope to sleep soundly at all this semester. A typical dorm mattress has been around longer than you have, is covered in vinyl, and feels lumpier than a hole-in-the-wall motel bed. They're not exactly conducive to a college student's much-needed beauty rest.

Mattress pads do much more than simply improve the comfort of your bed. They also protect the mattress and keep the sheets snugly in place. Like a fitted sheet, mattress pads cover the top and sides of the mattress. Because many universities use extra-long beds, an expandable "guaranteed-to-fit" pad is your best bet.

Pure-cotton mattress covers might cost more initially, but

### Mattress Pad

- A mattress pad isn't a dorm room luxury; it's a necessity.

- A fifteen-year-old bed has lumps and haywire springs. A nice mattress pad completely disguises these imperfections.

- Not only will it even out the irregularities and improve support, but a pad will make sleeping where so many people have slept before doable.

- The thicker and softer, the better. If possible buy one made of all natural fabrics like cotton, wool, or feathers.

### Foam Covers

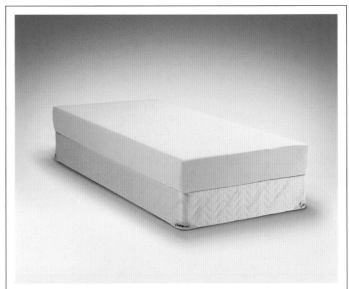

- A mattress topper lies on top of the bed under your bedding. It can be used in combination with a mattress pad to offer even more comfort.

- Memory foam, one of the most common mattress toppers, provides between one and four inches of cushioning. As time goes on, they conform to your body and remain temperature and weight sensitive.

- Mattress toppers improve support for your back and neck, reduce pressure points, and often prevent mold, mildew, and bed bugs. Yuck.

they'll last far longer than cotton/polyester blends. Wool is another good choice, as it naturally wicks away moisture. Mattress pads are machine washable and should be washed about half as often as you wash your sheets—which means your pad should make it in the laundry at least once a month.

A mattress encasement, which zips around the mattress and covers it completely, offers more protection (but less comfy padding) than a mattress pad. Depending on the product, some are simply waterproof, while others product from dust and dander.

## Egg Crates

- Convoluted mattress pads, commonly known as egg crates, are densely dimpled foam pads.

- They're designed to improve circulation, boost cushioning, and reduce tossing and turning.

- The open-cell bedding allows air to circulate, creating more comfortable sleeping temperatures.

- The only catch? Some people can't adjust to sleeping in a bumpy bed, intentionally or not.

## New Mattresses

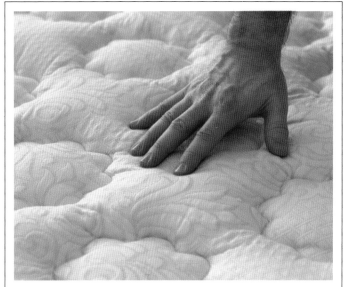

- Can you buy your own mattress? Sure. Do you need to? No way.

- Unless you plan to buy a twin bed when you move out of the dorm, don't invest in a new mattress simply to use for the year.

- The hassle just isn't worth the temporary comfort. You'll have to track down an extra-long mattress and find a place to store the university's mattress in the interim. Not worth it.

# BED SKIRTS

## Conceal your under-the-bed storage and dust bunnies in style

Bed skirts are traditionally designed to conceal a bed's box spring. In a dorm room, bed skirts serve a far more important purpose: to allow you to utilize your under-the-bed space as storage in a stylish way.

A bed skirt offers you another opportunity to inject color, patterns, and personality into your bedding. Most bedspreads and sheet sets have optional matching bed skirts,

but contrasting shades can add serious style. Because your under-the-bed storage needs to be easily accessible, skip tailored bed skirts and instead opt for ruffled or pleated.

Because dorm beds are typically well over 3 feet off the ground (as compared to a traditional bed's 16 to 18 inches), they require bed skirts with a minimum 24-inch "drop."

Such a long bed skirt is hard to come by. Look for "day bed

### Ruffled Bed Skirts

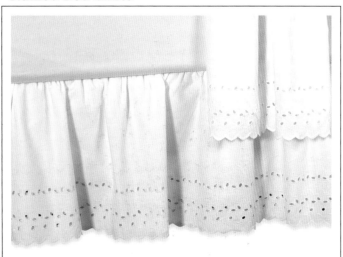

- Ruffled bed skirts, also known as dust ruffles, are the most common of their kind—but not necessarily the most stylish.

- They're fantastically convenient, because they allow easy access underneath the bed. Unfortunately they're a little too frilly for many young adults who prefer sleeker room decor.

- Pleated and zigzagged bed skirts make it just as easy to reach underneath, but much to the relief of college kids everywhere, look far less frou-frou.

### Pleated Bed Skirts

- Pleated bed skirts can be pleated throughout like the ruffled variation, but the more common style is tailored flat featuring kick pleats at the corners.

- Swapping ruffles for pleats creates a more sophisti-cated, less frilly alternative to the ruffled variety.

- Pleats are an ideal option for boys, who can't bear the thought of decorating their room with anything that resembles ruffles.

skirts" and "king-size dust ruffles," but if your search doesn't yield any results, just whip up your own with thread, a needle, and a long sheet of fabric. If your bedding set comes with a matching bed skirt, layer it over a longer variety or modify it with ribbons, ruffles, or an extra stripe of fabric.

## Curtains

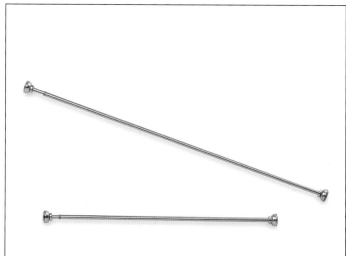

- Traditional bed skirts rest on the box springs, but if your bed is lifted *or* lofted, the skirt won't adequately cover your under-the-bed storage.

- A compression rod—or even an adjustable shower curtain rod—can be arranged to fit between the two outer posts of your bed.

- Many bedspreads have matching curtains and can be hemmed to the height of your bed to make a perfect bed skirt.

## Bed-Skirt Pockets

- If you don't have space for a bedside table, look to bed-skirt pockets or bedside caddies to stow your nighttime necessities.

- Designed specifically for dorms, bedside caddies cling to the mattress so your stuff is always within arm's reach.

- Sew a contrasting "pocket" onto your bed skirt. Cut a small piece of fabric in a square shape, hem the ends under, and stitch it right on your skirt.

- As a shortcut you can simply loop a small tote around your bedpost.

# DESKTOPS
## Make homework more enjoyable with a stylish desktop

Every dorm has the same desk: functional and sleek, but nothing fancy. Because this piece of furniture is such a focal point, a nifty desktop is necessary.

Color coordinating your desktop accessories creates a certain amount of continuity, and adding a colorful desk pad ties it all together. Anything from a dining room place mat to a flat panel of bright glass can make a nice study-ready surface.

The hutch of your desk is where you'll gaze during long stretches of strenuous assignments, so make it inspiring. Outfit it with a piece of cork so you can tack up anything that stimulates your imagination. Fitting the hutch with bright fabric or wrapping paper also brings a pop of color.

The less clutter you have within eyesight, the less distracted you'll be. Keep a few fabric-covered boxes around to catch

## Desk Sets

- Sleek matching desk sets include notebooks, storage units, and pen holders—all the necessities for a desk.

- Buy a color-coordinated set that includes everything you might need, or mix-and-match your own collection to coordinate with your room.

- Search office-supply stores for sophisticated ones. Leather varieties might cost more *now*, but they'll last you well into your career.

- You can cover all your desk supplies in contact paper and make a personalized desk set tailored to your taste.

## Slot Organizers

- Slot organizers, often intended to arrange mail, are a great way to manage your class assignments, notes, and exams.

- Look for smaller cabinets that can fit on your desktop without taking up too much valuable study space.

- Modular organizers make the most of your desk space, no matter how limited it may be.

- Test-tube holders are a clever way to keep your pens, pencils, and highlighters in tip-top shape.

bits and pieces that otherwise pile up on your work space.

Store an attractive shallow basket underneath your desk as a catchall. Magazine files, bookends, and letter trays also help with organization.

Mason jars and empty coffee cans are a playful way to store odds and ends in style. With polishing, they look nice and shiny, especially if you change up the lids with fabric.

Add a magnetic strip across your desk, then buy a few magnetic clips. Anytime you need to type up class notes or make edits to a paper, just clip it up for easy viewing.

## Desk Organizers

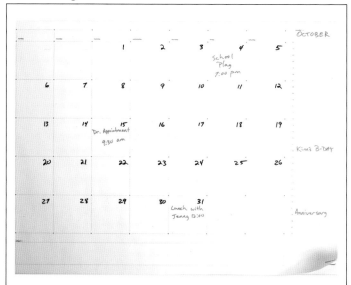

- Desktop organizers dress up your desktop and keep your meetings, classes, and obligations at your fingertips.

- The best desktop organizers have removable notepads and sticky notes that allow you to take your appointments with you.

- Make your own by attaching notepads to a poster board and decorating it with colorful paper, pens, and labels.

## Desktop Filing

- Desktop filing is perfect for keeping active files handy and is easily portable. The durable translucent polypropylene material can withstand everyday use while retaining its contemporary style.

- Loose-leaf binders with labels can keep everything organized, and you can store everything right on your desk shelf.

- If you have room for a file cabinet, toss a cool tablecloth or vintage silk scarf over the top and use it as a bedside table

# DRAWERS

## Store your stuff behind closed . . . drawers

Whatever you do, don't junk up your drawers with odds and ends. Organized, visually appealing drawers make your life infinitely easier and surprisingly more enjoyable (seriously!).

Something as simple as a cutlery tray can be used to stash your study essentials with ease, and they can be stacked up in deeper drawers to maximize the available space. Other unexpected drawer organizers include egg cartons, ice-cube trays, and short juice glasses.

Use small hooks to hang everything you can: Scissors, tape dispensers, and key chains can be dangled for simple grab-and-go.

Many office-supply stores sell prefilled desk trays that come stocked with sticky notes, paper clips, pushpins and other study necessities. Only buy these if you'll truly use everything

### Drawer Dividers

- Dividing your drawers—which are few and far between to begin with—will make the most of your drawer space. Spring-loaded dividers stay in place with handy tension rods.

- Drawer doublers, which can be stacked one on top of another, double (or triple, if your drawers are extra deep!) the space of each desk drawer.

- Desk drawers sometimes double as catch alls for small accessories, and diamond drawer dividers are ideal for grab-and-go things like gloves and scarves.

### Vanity Organizers

- Pens, pencils, and paper clips are easily lost in the depths of your desk drawers. Vanity organizers keep your study routine running smoothly.

- Expandable drawer organizers that hold items in place help with hasty drawer slamming (being in a hurry happens to everyone).

- Make your own organizers with unexpected household items like ice-cube trays, egg crates, and teacups. Not only are these things cheaper to buy, they're multipurpose so you can use them for years in different functions.

they include; otherwise you'll be wasting valuable money and space.

Line your drawers with contract paper, velvet fabric, or mirrors. Not only do they make ordinary drawer contents look appealing, they're also quite useful. Liners allow for easy cleanup of makeup spills, ink leaks, and other unforeseen accidents.

············· YELLOW ● LIGHT ·············

When your desktop fills up with papers, exams, and other odds and ends that don't seem to belong anywhere, you'll be tempted to push everything into your desk drawers. Resist this temptation. While this may be a quick fix, tackling piles as they accumulate is far more efficient. Delegate a spot for anything that needs to be kept, and trash everything that doesn't.

## Flatware Organizers

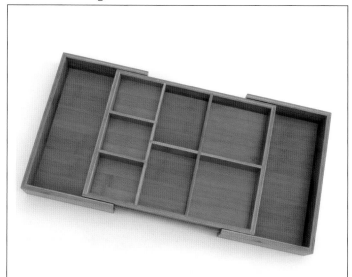

- Flatware organizers, intended for kitchen use, are every bit as helpful repurposed to fit desk drawers.

- Store pencils where knives go, scissor in the wooden spoon slot, and paper clips in the napkin-ring slot.

- These organizers can be stacked to maximize your space, and they're dishwasher safe (not that dorms have dishwashers, but that'll come in useful one day).

## Compartmentalizing

- Mini loaf pans, which can be purchased for a little more than a dollar apiece, can compartmentalize your drawers.

- Keep them in place with a touch of sticky tack on the bottom.

- Mini muffin tins are cool

enough to store *outside* of your drawers. Line them with pretty contact paper, and use them to store trinkets on top of your desk.

- Other compartmentalizing possibilities include small cardboard boxes and little plastic tubs from kitchen leftovers.

# DESK LIGHTING
## Shed light on your studying by investing in high-quality desk lamps

When it comes to desk lighting, look for something that's functional and fashionable. It should provide a fair amount of light, take up little surface space, and have an adjustable component.

Lamps should have the ability to be adjusted downward, casting light directly on your work—instead of directly into your eyes. Staring at a bare bulb will only agitate study sessions; indirect lighting prevents headaches and aids concentration.

Key terms to keep in mind when searching for a desk lamp are "pantograph arms" and "adjustable head," which basically mean that they can be arranged to your liking.

Look for a nice desk lamp that can double as bedside light. Let's face it, your room isn't big enough to necessitate both,

### Clip-On Lamps

- Book lamps clip directly onto your textbook for go-anywhere studying. They can also be clipped to your desk or bed.

- The contraption looks wonderfully high tech, but it's deceivingly simple to use. Typically battery operated, you don't have to deal with charging the battery or changing the bulb.

- These can be found for just over $2, but don't buy the cheapest available. A mid-range lamp is much more worth your money because the light will last longer.

### Built-In Desk Lamps

- Many dorm desks come equipped with a dim built-in light. While this certainly is a convenient addition, the harsh glare will pain your eyes after awhile.

- Add your own desk lamp without taking up any surface space with a clip-on light.

- A strand of rope lights, which can usually be found around the holidays, can illuminate your desk brilliantly.

so you might as well find one that serves duel purposes.

Touch-base lamps that allow you to adjust the brightness with the touch of a finger are worth the investment. Fancy clap lights *sound* convenient, but they're much more entertaining than they are efficient.

## LED Lamps

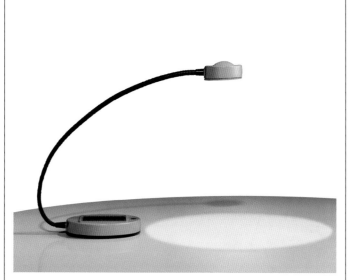

- LED lamps provide the same amount of light as a 40W incandescent with a much more soothing glow.

- Not only is the crisp light less stressful on your eyes, it's less stressful on the environment, too. LED lights consume less than a quarter of the electricity and last nearly three times the amount of traditional bulbs.

- You help the environment, but you do yourself a service, too. Slower-burning bulbs mean fewer replacements.

## Antique Desk Lamps

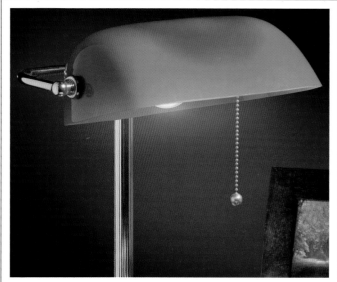

- If you want to bring a bit of poise to your dorm decor, skip the high-tech desk lamp and opt for the venerable "banker's lamp."

- An authentic banker's lamp has a brass base and green glass-shaded lamp.

- The green glass shade gives off a soft glow, and many originals simply require regular bulbs.

- If you can't dig up a vintage banker's lamp, reproductions abound. Look for different colors and funky patterned glass shades.

# DESK CHAIRS
## The key to scholarly success? A comfy desk chair

Dorm rooms come with desk chairs, but if you plan to spend a considerable amount of time studying there, think about sending your desk chair home with your parents and investing in one that's more conducive to sitting for hours on end. Keep in mind that the chair will need to be returned to the residence hall at the end of the year.

If you spend a lot of time at your desk, this expense will be worth the long-term investment. When searching for a new desk chair, look for buzz words like "adjustable" and "ergonomically correct."

Because your dorm room more than likely has hard floors, wheels allow you to slide around to situate yourself. Casters are a must. Whether you choose a sleek computer chair or a classic swivel armchair, the luxury of rolling around adds to

### Computer Chairs

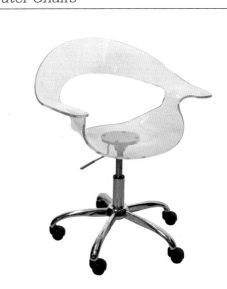

- Computer chairs, also known as task chairs, are specifically designed for office use for their attractive design and comfortable feel.

- Most are designed with the intention of remaining comfortable for those who work hours on end—ideal for any dedicated scholar.

- The swivel seat, reclining back, and "gas lift" that allows you to raise and lower yourself will adapt to any desk. They also allow you to change positions if you get uncomfortable midway through a study session.

### Executive Chairs

- A classic leather (or faux leather) chair adds an impossible amount of style to such a small space.

- These can be found for reasonable prices at office supply stores and off-price retailers like TJ Maxx and Marshalls.

- Look for key details like leather tufting, cushioned armrests, and wood trim.

- Another similarly sleek option is a traditional dining chair, which could be found at a second-hand shop for less than $50.

78

the experience. If your room comes with carpet, or you plan on placing an accent rug underneath your desk, a plastic chair mat enables spinning, rotating, and rolling.

The ideal desk chair is completely subjective, but great support is nonnegotiable. If your back and neck aren't comfortable, find something else—and fast.

If your dorm chair is just fine, dress it up with new cushions, decorative pillows, or slipcovers. Or just throw a coordinating blanket around the back of the chair for a cozy addition.

## Chair Pillows and Slipcovers

- A few cushions and a slipcover can make a world of difference with a school-provided desk chair.

- Don't seek out fancy slipcovers for such a simple chair. Throwing on a fantastic tapestry can completely transform it.

- Up the comfort level with a supportive pillow. Oversize accent pillows look *and* feel great, and armchair pillows are a perfect fit.

## Cushioned Armchairs

- A classic family room–style armchair is surprisingly efficient as a dorm room desk chair.

- It can serve two purposes at once: Pulled up to the desk, it can stand in as office seating; flipped away from your desk, it can be your cozy lounge chair.

- If you choose to use an armchair, buy a style that does not sit too far back, because hunching forward for hours on end will literally kill your back.

# COMPUTERS

## As a college student, nothing connects you to campus—and to home—quite like a computer

Of all the gadgets you can buy for college, a computer should be first and foremost on your list of must-haves. You can watch TV, play video games, and write impressive papers with just one trusty electronic.

The luxury of an in-room computer allows you to work on homework and catch up on important e-mails when it's convenient for you. Most universities have student discounts or special back-to-school deals.

If a computer is not in your budget, never fear. Dorms have computer lab accessibility throughout the day and sometimes into the late night. Campus libraries are stocked with more than enough computers and often have laptops

### Desktop

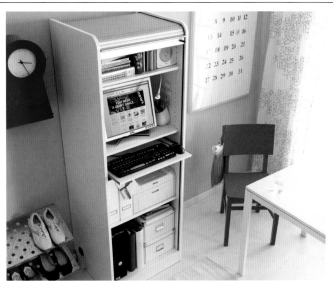

- Desktop computers are less expensive and longer lasting than their mobile counterparts. What they possess in value, they lack in convenience.

- You can't take your desktop computer to class, you can't lug it to the library, and

you can't work away from your dorm room even if your roommate is throwing a raging party the night before your twenty-page term paper is due.

- If you happen to be exceedingly accident-prone, desktops are brilliant.

### Laptop and Notebook Computers

- Laptops have a shorter shelf life than desktop computers, but they make a college student's life indescribably easier.

- You can take notes in a Word document during class, study those notes at the library, then print them out to review before the exam.

- You can use your computer everywhere from the common room to the corner park.

- Take considerable care of your laptop and always properly transport it in a padded laptop case. *Never* toss it in your backpack along with your textbooks.

available to "rent" for a few hours. You'll have to manage your time more wisely than your laptop-equipped friends—no starting your paper the night before it's due for you!—but you'll be a better student for it.

## Computer Printer

- A printer is convenient to have around the room for late-night revisions and early morning study guides, but it certainly isn't a necessity.

- If you're keeping a close eye on your budget, skip the printer and take advantage of the printing opportunities on campus.

- Many schools include a printing budget in their yearly campus fees.

- Using campus printers means you don't have to worry about supplying your own paper or ink.

## Computer Accessories

- A wireless keyboard allows you to type from up to thirty feet away from your monitor, so whether you use a desktop or laptop, you can get cozy while writing that twenty-page paper.

- Because laptops are so conveniently portable—and thus prone to accidents— saving your files on an external hard drive offers serious insurance.

- Web cams are another computer add-on that are worth the splurge. A simple setup allows you to video chat with family and friends all over the world.

# MAKESHIFT DESKS

## Step away from your dorm-room desk and get to work on a clever alternative

When you need to give your dorm-room desk a rest, turn to a makeshift surface to get things done. From accent tables to collapsible trays, anything with a steady surface and streamlined shape is a smart substitute to your drab desk.

Peekaboo accent tables, also called half-moon or C-shaped desks, can roll right up to your bed. These can be found everywhere from furniture stores to hospital suppliers—in fact, the utilitarian adjustable table used in hospitals looks incredibly cool after a thick coat of paint. Tray tables with X-shaped bases fold completely flat, and the versatile top can also be used as a desk tray. Carts on wheels—typically used in kitchens, bathrooms, and nurseries—make

### Desk Tray

- Desk trays, also known as lap desks, are ideal if you spend a lot of time on your bed surrounded by textbooks.

- Although the concept is the same, the difference between the two lies in the design. Whereas the desk

tray sits over your legs like a miniature table, the lap desk has a soft pillow base that rests right on your lap.

- Opt for a wooden surface over a plastic one; it's easier to write on and better for your laptop computer's circulation.

### Lazy Susans

- If you don't want to spend money on a lap desk, look around the house for similar surfaces that can be repurposed as a study table.

- Lazy Susans—originally intended for kitchen use—are strong enough to hold notebooks, textbooks, and laptops.

- Lazy Susans come in tons of colors and have a swivel top that can rotate as needed.

- Also look into cutting boards and breakfast-in-bed serving trays. Both have substantial surface areas, can be stored flat, and are useful to have on hand later in life.

phenomenal mobile desks. As a bonus, most boast extra shelving.

Makeshift desks are much more efficient than resting your notebook or laptop directly on your bed, which is far too flexible to serve as a writing surface and can overheat your computer.

### Serving Cart

- A rolling serving cart, similar to something you might see at a restaurant, is an exceptional addition for a dorm.

- Use the top surface as a desk and the lower shelves to store textbooks, binders, and other study supplies.

- Serving carts can be found at kitchen-supply stores. Nursery changing tables, a similar piece of furniture with a very different intended use, works equally well.

- The best part is that these makeshift tables don't need chairs—just push them right up to your bed!

### Antique School Desk

- Look through vintage stores for antique school desks. Because they're small and compact in shape, they can squeeze into a dorm room with ease.

- A school desk is a nice reprieve from your dorm's existing desk, and the storage under the tabletop can hold all your books and supplies.

- These antique desks go for about $50 on eBay and are cool pieces to hold onto for years to come.

# STORAGE
## Stash your stuff in stylish bins, steamer trunks, and more

To keep your dorm room from turning into a utilitarian storage unit, stash your belongings in stylish containers. Living out of boxes may seem like the easiest option upon moving in, but it will not simplify your life.

Organization can double task as decoration if it's presented in the right way. Make sure everything in your room has a designated place. Corral your clutter with brightly colored milk crates. Store last season's clothes in a translucent plastic crate.

Stylish alternatives abound if you look past classic containers like plastic tubs. Stash pillows and blankets in a steamer trunk—and use it as a coffee table when friends stop by.

Stacked in a tier of two or three, vintage suitcases can conceal clothing, blankets, and other seasonal extras; plus they add chic surface space. The suitcases don't need to match

### Milk Crates

- Milk crates from actual milk-processing plants—think black, red, or blue palate with an old-school brand stamp—look cheeky and cool.

- You can also buy brand-new crates made of a lighter-weight plastic and in bright, decor-friendly colors.

- Classic milk crates are made of wire or wooden slats. Though neither are as strong as the modern variety, they look great as storage.

- Milk crate-style baskets are a fresh alternative to plastic ones, and the liners can be easily removed for laundering.

### Plastic Bins

- Plastic storage bins, similar to the kind you stashed your toys in as a kid, add a bright shot of primary color to your drab dorm room.

- Not only do they stack, they can also be stored on a thin wooden rack if you can spare the floor space.

- Plain clear plastic tubs are viable storage options, but they're best hidden under the bed.

- Shallow bins are great for clothes, while deep ones work for blankets, pillows, and larger objects.

(which would be a near-impossible feat when dealing with vintage carryalls). Look for similarly colored pieces of luggage, and stack from largest to smallest.

Turn any ol' container into a stylish storage space with the help of contact paper, spray paint, and a little creativity. A boost of bright color can transform cardboard boxes, wicker baskets, and cheap plastic tubs into something special with a touch of DIY design.

## Steamer Trunks

- Steamer trunks have a heftier price tag, but they last years and withstand serious use.

- These old-fashioned crates stylishly store everything from clothes to blankets to sporting equipment.

- They're incredibly sleek, so there's no need to hide steamer trunks under the depths of your bed.

- Keep the trunk out and make use of it—simply toss floor pillows around it and you've got a coffee table.

### Shopping through the Kids' Department

- Your professors will love to remind you that you're an adult now, but that doesn't mean you can't shop in the kids' department.

- A treasure trove of colorful furniture and pint-size storage, kids' home goods are also cheaper.

- Balance your more whimsical decorations with sophisticated basics.

ORGANIZING

# MEMO BOARDS
## Reminders and memorabilia are repurposed as pretty wall decor

When you're constantly on the go, it can be difficult to keep track of your most important obligations, lists, and messages. With a colorful memo board prominently displaying your duties, however, you'll never miss another appointment, class, or date again.

Corkboards are convenient because you can tack up notes, photographs, and postcards, and rearrange to please. All you really need is a sheet of cork and a handful of pushpins. If you're feeling crafty, cover the cork in fabric and make your own decorative pin board.

Pegboards, the perforated alternative to corkboards, can be used to tack up everything from clocks to calendars. They're especially ideal for jewelry—use hooks and loops to store (and display!) pretty necklaces, bracelets, and earrings.

### Corkboards

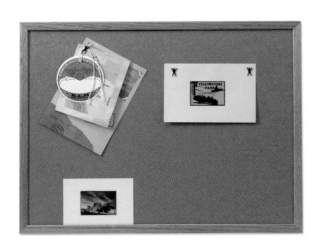

- Bright pushpins make all the difference when you're tacking up less-than-exciting things like exam reviews.

- Decorate your corkboard with a little paint and a lot of creativity.

- Consider cutting a piece of corkboard into shapes, like circles or diamonds, for instant wall decor.

- Make your own fabric-covered corkboard using colors that coordinate with your bedding.

### Chalkboards

- Desktop chalkboards are a stylish way to keep reminders in plain view.

- If your dorm gives you the okay to use paint on your walls, consider chalkboard paint. No need to paint the entire room—a wall or even just a rectangle will suffice.

- You can rescue oversize chalkboards—like those used in elementary schools—from vintage stores.

Dry—erase boards are perfect for communicating with your roommate when you're both on the go and in and out of the room. Chalkboards serve the same purpose, in a much more old-school way. If you don't mind the dust, chalkboards look cool and add a slick vintage style element. If allowed, paint a wall with dry-erase or chalkboard paint for an entire wall of memos and doodles.

## MAKE IT EASY

Think outside the box when it comes to memo boards. One idea is to attach a serving tray to the wall with removable adhesives for an unexpectedly stylish wall decoration. Old-fashioned silver-plated serving trays happen to be magnetic, so you can tack up your important memos with ease.

### Dry-Erase Boards

- Dry-erase boards are the less dusty, more modern version of chalkboards.

- Look for dry-erase boards intended for school lockers—they have adhesive backs that are safe for walls.

- If you have a minifridge, cover the front with a magnetic dry-erase board and make grocery lists.

- Dry-erase paint can be used for more than just the walls. Try it on any hard surface, like picture frames, storage bins, and trash cans.

### Peg Boards

- A piece of peg board can be affixed to the wall with adhesives, or you can slip a piece over the back of your desk for built-in storage.

- Peg-board hooks, found at any hardware store, can stash everything from tote bags to necklaces.

- You can find peg board in white, but the classic brown takes to spray paint very well.

- Cut a piece of peg board the size of your desk's hutch and use it for study aids, exam reminders . . . and fun snapshots of friends!

# OVER-THE-DOOR STORAGE

## Turn an underappreciated door into an additional "closet"

Over-the-door pockets can store everything from shoes to school supplies to T-shirts. The only caveat? The number of doors in a dorm room is limited, so you really have to take a look at your own possessions to see what sort of space is more in demand.

There's an endless amount of over-the-door racks and a very limited amount of space, so look for organizers with multiple uses. Pocket storage is typically intended for shoes, but can also accommodate scarves, belts, even neatly rolled up T-shirts. If your wardrobe isn't that expansive, over-the-door pockets work well for bath and beauty products.

Yet another option? Create a mobile kitchen and store cooking supplies, canned food, and packaged snacks in these multipurpose pockets.

### Over-the-Door Pockets

- Don't use over-the-door pockets just for shoes— these handy pouches are the perfect size for important belongings that get lost in the bustle of a dorm.

- Look for sturdier materials like canvas so you can stuff more *stuff* into them.

- Use a half-and-half system, delegating only the bottom half for shoes.

- The top half can store daily necessities, like bath products, school supplies, and hats and gloves.

### Storage Systems

- A little more sophisticated than their pocket counterpart, over-the-door storage systems manage to look sleek while holding a lot of stuff.

- Look for floor-to-ceiling varieties for maximum storage space; adjustable shelves are another big plus.

- The most common over-the-door storage system is made from white vinyl-coated steel. Put your own stamp on it with a coat of bright paint.

Streamlined hooks can hang backpacks, sweatshirts, and jackets. The more hooks, the better. Combine a few different storage varieties to make the most of the whole 32 x 80-inch door. Aside from under the bed, the door is one of the most valuable slices of storage in a small dorm room.

*Over-the-Door Hooks*

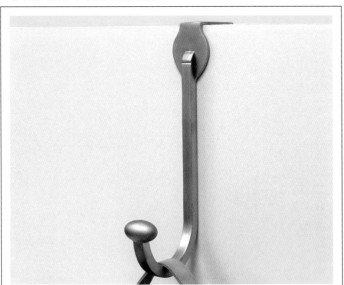

- Install over-the-door hooks on your dorm-room door and hang jackets, umbrellas, and school bags that you can grab before you head to class.

- If you have a closet door, these hooks come in handy for clothes that seem to end up on the floor instead of in the hamper.

- Hooks can be purchased as a unit or individually, so they can be successfully combined with other over-the-door organizers.

*Over-the-Door Hat Rack*

- Essentially a door full of hooks, over-the-door hat racks can be used for more than a baseball cap collection.

- Hang scarves, sweaters, and towels on the tier of hooks. They're pretty perfect for handbags too.

- Because they're so narrow, hat racks can be doubled up or used in combination with another over-the-door organizer.

- Of all the over-the-door options, hat racks are by far the coolest. Filled with a collection of caps, they make a dorm room look athletic.

ORGANIZING

# HOOKS

## Everything looks cooler—and is more compact—hanging from a hook

The number one necessity for an enjoyable dorm experience is a comfy place to catch up on your z's. The number two? Wall hooks. Never underestimate this all-encompassing, incredibly handy accessory that has the uncanny ability to turn *anything* into a wall decoration.

The way to make wall hooks look like intended decor instead of haphazard storage is to combine a handful of same-size hooks in clusters or rows.

If nails are allowed, use hooks to their full potential. One cluster can corral jewelry, another can hold keys; one bunch can hold scarves and accessories, another towels and other shower necessities.

### Clothesline Collages

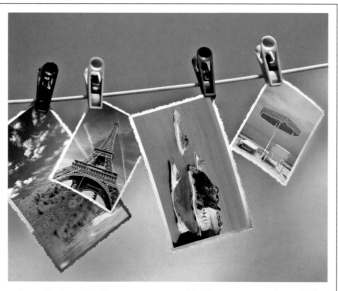

- Install a laundry line across your wall for a wonderful display of anything that tickles your fancy.

- Make it part of your decor, and pin up postcards, posters, and pictures.

- Use it as a memo board of sorts and post class notes, reminders, bills, and other documents you need to keep safe.

### Wall Hook Options

- The hardware store is filled with hooks of all sizes and finishes. Even a tool novice can hammer these into walls with ease.

- Adhesive hooks can be used to hang pretty knickknacks for decorative purposes or clothes and accessories for utilitarian purposes.

- Before attaching plastic hooks to the wall, test them out on an inconspicuous spot—on certain surfaces they might leave a sticky residue.

- Check the label to see how much weight each hook can hold.

If nails *aren't* allowed, stock up on removable adhesive hooks. They aren't as pretty as the sleek metal varieties, but the clear plastic will blend into any light-colored wall. Even better? They now make stylish plastic hooks *look* like metal.

Wall hooks can also be used as a pretty alternative to framed pictures and posters. Simply run a piece of ribbon through the back of the frame, tie a bow, and hang it from a hook.

## Clothespins

- Classic dime-store clothespins can be directly attached to the wall with sticky adhesives.

- Use them to pin anything from photographs to jewelry, or use them to artfully hang posters and snapshots.

- Wooden clothespins take to paint even better than their plastic counterparts, so give them a few coats of bright paint and pattern them in an equally intense contrasting color.

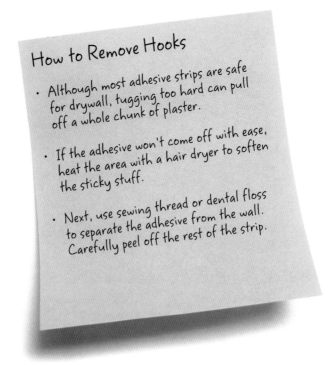

How to Remove Hooks

- Although most adhesive strips are safe for drywall, tugging too hard can pull off a whole chunk of plaster.

- If the adhesive won't come off with ease, heat the area with a hair dryer to soften the sticky stuff.

- Next, use sewing thread or dental floss to separate the adhesive from the wall. Carefully peel off the rest of the strip.

ORGANIZING

# SHELVING
## Nothing beats shelves for storage *and* style

When you have more wall space than floor space, shelving can increase your surface area by tenfold.

Look for shelves that can be expanded or added onto as needed. Interlocking wire cubes attach at the corners for stacking options. A set of four can be turned into a larger four-cubby cube or stacked to make a vertical multishelf unit. These often come in myriad colors—especially if you peek

around the kids' department of a home store.

If you don't love the look of wire, look for a similar shelving system made of cedar or walnut wood, typically sold in separate units. Start out with a few cubes and work your way up as needed. Around a foot in length, these take up very little floor space and can be stacked to the ceiling for serious storage.

### Desk Shelves

- Make the most of your desk's few shelves with clever organization. Everything should have a use and its own place.

- Stacking shelves, found in many kitchen-supply stores, can be added on to desk shelves.

- Under-the-shelf organizers, also found in the kitchen section, are sized surprisingly well to stash papers, binders, and other must-save documents.

- Acrylic shelf dividers double the storage and keep things where they're supposed to be.

### Corner Shelves

- Make the most of empty corners by installing small shelving units. These shelves act as great display areas, but can also store books and binders.

- Keep an eye out for shelves that are tall but thin—thus

taking up little floor area and maximizing vertical space.

- A corner shelf would be relatively simple to make with a few flat boards and two pie-shaped pieces of wood.

Shop outside the home-organization department for cool shelving alternatives. Add cupboard shelves to a dresser, slide a spice rack on a desk, and clip a bedside ledge to the bed.

**ZOOM**

If you are among the lucky few who dwell in dorms that give nails and screws the okay, hack away and hammer in shelves to build up your vertical storage. Wall shelves can be stacked in rows or staggered to create visual interest. Use them to display knickknacks and store books, handbags, and even shoes!

## Cube Shelving

- Start small when it comes to cube shelving. Buy a few cubes to begin with, and then add on as needed as the year goes on.

- The appeal of cubes is that they can be stacked and expanded as needed while still looking stylish.

- Cube shelving can be constructed from milk crates, stacked on their sides with the enclosed bottoms toward the wall.

## Bedside Storage

- Be crafty to come up with a bedside table. Try arranging your room to accommodate a surface by moving your bed near the window ledge or top shelf of your desk for a built-in tabletop.

- Because there isn't always room for a bedside table, a small bedside shelf gives you a nice ledge to store necessities like a book, glass of water, and cell phone.

- Another option? Try hanging a shallow over-the-door shelf on the frame of your bed for instant storage.

93

# MAINTAINING ORGANIZATION
## Keeping a dorm room in tip-top shape

It's important to thoroughly organize your room upon moving in, but it's even more important to maintain that organization as the year goes on. The only way to keep things in tip-top shape is to take some time for upkeep every week or two.

Unpacking is the easy part; maintaining order is where things get tough. Even with the best intentions, clutter accumulates. Take an hour or two each week to reorganize. Everything that's out of place should be returned to it's proper spot, and if it doesn't have a place to go, consider tossing it (or finding a new home for it).

Carefully labeling your storage containers is the only way to maintain organization . . . *and* your sanity. Use decorative labels and detail the contents, focusing on the things you'll be looking for again and again. You may *think* you'll remember

### *Organizing Schoolwork*

- Papers have a way of piling up in the most overwhelming way.

- All of sudden you have a stack of papers twenty deep and you don't know what needs to be saved, what can be tossed, and what should have been turned in two weeks ago.

- Immediately file everything into its appropriate folders or files, and trash anything you no longer need—but only things you're *sure* you won't need, because old tests and papers have a way of resurfacing.

### *Organizing Bedding*

- Making a bed can make your room look infinitely more well kept—even if it's concealing dirty clothes and last night's pizza boxes underneath.

- Tuck in your sheet, smooth your comforter, and for the final touch, fluff your pillow.

- If making your bed is just too much trouble, lose the top sheet and sleep with a duvet that's easy to smooth out.

where you stored your winter boots, but when a snowstorm hits and you have to make it to class in twenty minutes, you'll find yourself dumping the contents of every container in the middle of your dorm-room floor. Have catchalls like wall pockets, expandable pouches, file folders, and a junk drawer or two.

No matter how diligent you are about throwing your clothes in the hamper, making your bed, and cleaning dirty dishes, your roommate has the prerogative to live like a complete slob. If roomie turns his or her side of the room into a total pigsty, offer to share your cleaning supplies and gently suggest a few hours of housekeeping. If all else fails, install room curtains.

## Organizing Clothes

- A typical college day calls for multiple outfit changes: sweats for class, jeans for dinner, a dress for dancing, and pj's for bed.

- To keep the discarded clothes off your floor and in your closet, immediately toss anything that's dirty into a hamper.

- Slide anything that's still clean (or even clean-ish) back on a hanger.

**The Importance of Labels**

- Use labels for storage-container descriptions or to add your name to DVDs, CDs, and books.

- Label things you don't want to share: Tag food in the fridge and toiletries in the bathroom.

- No need to buy a label maker. Use a set of nice labels and a calligraphy pen to make even better-looking labels.

ORGANIZING

# SEATING
## Sitting in style . . . even on the floor

Colorful, comfortable, and surprisingly convenient seating can turn any day in the dorm into an impromptu party.

To make your habitat hang-out friendly, a handful of chairs will have suitemates clamoring to snag a seat in your room. Keep two or three on hand, and stash them away until your friends come knocking. With extra seating available, your space will be the go-to place for TV-watching parties, late-night movie marathons, informal dinner festivities, and around-the-clock study groups.

No one wants to lounge on a cold dorm floor, no matter how great the crowd is, and a bed only fits so many friends. People are drawn to places they feel welcome, so a spare chair or two will show fellow students just how hospitable you are.

### Director's Chairs

- Because director's chairs are usually covered with durable canvas, they can withstand spills.

- You can also buy slipcovers to create a much more cozy seat.

- These chairs are a classic, stylistically speaking, but they're also extremely useful.

- Director's chairs can fold up for simple storage and be pulled out of hiding with ease.

### Butterfly Chairs

- Also designed in sphere and dish figures, these modernist chairs bring futuristic style into a traditional dorm room.

- The portability and compact size allow these foldable chairs to move from room to room with ease.

- The cozy shape is ideal for curling up with a textbook—or your favorite magazine.

- Oversize varieties fit two comfortably, and classic stainless steel frames can withstand even more.

There's no need to stick to old folding chairs in an effort to save space; there are savvy furniture options that are as stylish as they are sensible. If space is an issue—and in a dorm room, it typically is—look for furniture that can be stored with ease. Beanbags can be stashed under the bed, floor pillows stack up nicely, and butterfly chairs fold up to the size of an umbrella. For rooms that have extra floor space, armchairs, sleeper chairs, or loveseats are indispensable additions.

## Floor Pillows

- A stack of floor pillows makes for a fabulous makeshift bed. Add a few blankets, and you'll be hosting sleepovers in no time.

- Collect varying sizes, fabrics, and patterns—a few florals and polka dots for the girls; a few solid colors and stripes for the guys.

- Canvas cushions will last through hours of pillow fights, while machine-washable cotton pillows will hold up against your spill-prone friends.

- When in doubt buy doggie beds. Not only are they surprisingly comfortable, but they're pleasingly affordable.

## Sleeper Chairs

- Not only is the sleeper chair great for guests, it is the go-to seating for studying and napping.

- Don't have extra floor space? Loft your bed and store a sleeper chair underneath.

- Any old chair would work; simply swath it with a new seat cover.

ENTERTAINING

# MAKESHIFT TABLES
## Tabletops and stylish surfaces for small spaces

Whether you're planning dinner parties or board-game soirees, a reliable makeshift table is a must. When the alternative is the cold tile floor, anything suffices, but when there are so many stylish options, there's no reason to settle.

When you first move in, the rug may look like as great a place as any for spontaneous card games and TV-watching parties. After a few weeks of being trampled on by muddy boots and grimy socks, however, the rug looks progressively less inviting.

Additional surface space is a worthy addition if you hope to do any sort of entertaining, but that doesn't mean you need to invest in a brand-new table. Good thing, because you won't have the space for it in your little dorm room, anyway. TV trays, storage ottomans, and serving carts can all be used as spur-of-the-moment tabletops.

## Card Tables

- Card tables are nice enough to leave out all the time, but if you just need something for spur-of-the-moment get-togethers, they will get the job done.

- If you do buy a card table, look for a fun tablecloth to top it with. It will change the entire look and really add festive fun no matter how small the occasion.

- Because card tables are high enough to warrant chairs, simply gather desk chairs from your friends' rooms instead of buying an additional set of seats.

## TV Trays

- TV trays, once reserved for dinners in front of the tube, are fantastic for dorm rooms because of their clever fold-up capabilities.

- Instead of settling on flimsy plastic, look for rich wood— walnut turns a TV tray into a stylish piece of furniture.

- Most TV trays sit close to table height, making them perfect for a bedside surface (and they can moonlight as a nightstand!).

Think outside the box—or the rectangle, rather—when it comes to finding a tabletop. Literally anything, from a cardboard box to a plastic crate to a wooden stool, can be covered with a tablecloth and used as a table.

**ZOOM**

If you're feeling crafty, dig out an old camping cot, clean it off, fancy it up with bright paint, and reuse it as a card table. It's the perfect height paired with a handful of floor pillows. Plus it costs next to nothing and can be stashed under the bed.

## Storage Ottomans

- These clever little stools can be used as seating *or* surface space.

- Even better, they usually contain a nicely concealed storage space in the middle.

- Storage ottomans are typically cube shaped, making them optimal for stacking.

## Butler Trays

- Similar to a TV tray but much more stylish, the butler tray is definitely nice enough to leave out around the clock.

- The tray is removable, allowing easy cleanup, and the legs are completely collapsible for convenient storage.

- Can't seem to find a butler table? Look through the outdoor furniture department of your local home-improvement store.

ENTERTAINING

# GAMES
## All work and no play? Not in college

No matter what your college friends are like, chances are they'll love board games. Even if they don't openly admit to a love for, say, Monopoly, everyone has a weakness for board games bred from a childhood filled with Sorry! and Clue.

Despite the fact that these throwbacks to childhood don't have the hippest reputation, board games are a great way to get to know friends of friends and floormates you might not otherwise meet during the course of the semester.

Kind of like a rousing round of pickup basketball, board games bring out the competitive spirit in everyone. This adds to the fun, until someone storms out of the dorm muttering about cheaters and conspiracies. Keep everyone on speaking terms by balancing skill-based games like Monopoly with chance-based games like Uno.

### Strategy and Smarts Games

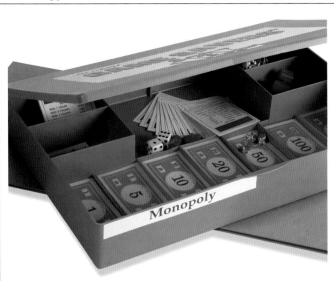

- Monopoly, a classic board game that can take more than three hours to finish, is great for groups of eight or fewer.

- Trivial Pursuit, another mainstay, is America's favorite trivia game for a reason—4,800 questions will keep the entertainment going for hours.

- Cranium is the new Trivial Pursuit: fast moving, fun, and, above all, challenging.

### Card Games

- A deck or two of cards provide endless entertainment. Learn the rules for basic games like Go Fish, Spoons, and Hearts. Know them well enough to teach newbies to play too.

- Be cautious of gambling—don't play games revolving around wagers of money. Like alcohol, many campuses have zero tolerance for gambling.

- Although it isn't a traditional card game, Uno is entertaining, addictive, and easy to store.

Lively games—Dominos and Jenga are particularly exciting—are a great way to spend an evening, especially if you make a night out of it by turning it into a party. Invite friends (and their friends!), set out snacks, and decorate with streamers and holiday lights.

ZOOM

Board games can take up a significant amount of space. Instead of stacking them horizontally, slide game boxes behind a dresser or stack them under your bed.

## Skill Games

- Jenga is endlessly entertaining, and the short fifteen-minute games are conveniently brief.

- Like cards, a set of dominos can be used to play a handful of games. Draw is the classic dominos game, but

Mexican Train is another group-friendly classic.

- Twister is a favorite of many young adults. This hilarious game is a fast way to get to know a whole floor of fellow students.

### Party Games

- Apples to Apples is a conversation-sparking game for groups of four to ten people. Once named "Party Game of the Year," Apples to Apples can last about an hour—although you are likely to play much longer than that.

- A team game that allows for an endless number of players, Catchphrase guarantees laughs and loud shouts—all the makings of a successful game night.

- Balderdash, which means "trivial nonsense" by definition, is about pretending you're smarter than you really are (college in a nutshell).

ENTERTAINING

101

# CHILLING OUT

## Give the books a break and take a chill pill

Sometimes you just have to kick back and hang out with your friends. Turn your room into the go-to haunt by making it a cool, comfortable place to be.

Start by tossing a few extra blankets on your bed. Not only will this protect your bedding, but friends will feel comfortable making themselves cozy. Make your bed even more homey with a high-quality bed cover or egg crate.

A variety of pillows in different shapes and sizes makes a bed look more like a stylish couch; bright pillows in soft materials warm a cold dorm room right up.

Forget the overhead fluorescent fixtures; a cluster of lamps brings much-needed mood lighting to a dorm room. Don't let December have all the fun—keep your Christmas lights up year-round.

### Music

- Load your iPod with songs of every genre and create playlists to suit every mood.

- Unless you have a huge CD collection, skip the boom box and save space with speakers for your MP3 player.

- Keep your iPod charged up and encourage friends to play DJ.

- Classic music aficionados will appreciate vintage record players. Not only do they play some of the best oldies around, but they add serious style to a desktop.

### Movies

- Keep a variety of DVDs in your room—college kids love television series on DVDs, which make perfect marathons after a day of studying.

- Store your DVDs in binders, shoebox-size containers, or desk drawers.

- Actual shoeboxes work, too. Simply cover them with decorative contact paper or create a collage with magazine cutouts.

102

A dorm room should be stocked with things that appeal to fellow students: an abundance of movies, music, and more than enough snacks to go around. Anytime you aren't busy, flip on the TV or blast your favorite tunes and keep your dorm-room door propped open. A wide-open door always encourages people to stop in to hang out.

## *Extra Pillows and Blankets*

- Extra stacks of pillows and blankets instantly warm up any room.

- Be prepared for unexpected drop-ins: Stash the pillow you sleep on, and cover your bed with fun throw pillows.

- Instead of thousands of tiny pillows, buy three or four oversize ones in similar color schemes and varying patterns.

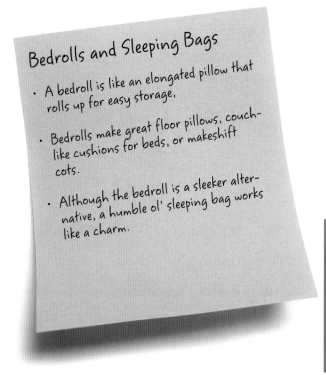

### Bedrolls and Sleeping Bags

- A bedroll is like an elongated pillow that rolls up for easy storage.

- Bedrolls make great floor pillows, couch-like cushions for beds, or makeshift cots.

- Although the bedroll is a sleeker alternative, a humble ol' sleeping bag works like a charm.

ENTERTAINING

# PARTIES

Movie marathons, game night, and other excuses to party hardy

The reality of college isn't quite like National Lampoon's party-hardy *Animal House,* but having a vibrant social life is just as important as having a valuable scholarly experience.

Your dorm room may be small, but it can be the setting of legendary parties. Just think of all the neighbors you can invite, all the movies you can watch, all the games you can play!

Plan a party in advance, and get the okay from your roommate. Written invitations are a nice touch, especially when simply slipped under the door, but e-mail invites and Web events are just as acceptable (and even more expedient).

Decorate with fun holiday lights, festive bowls of snacks, and plenty of pillows. If your party has a theme, alter the decor accordingly.

## Movie Night

- For a proper movie night, you need more than one flick on hand. Rent an original and a sequel for extended viewing.

- Try an entire trilogy for an epic movie marathon. *The Godfather, The Lord of the Rings,* and *Star Wars* are great triple threats.

- Scary movies are particularly successful, especially in creepy old residence halls.

## TV Night

- If all your friends love the same show, invite everyone over to tune in together.

- Come up with a menu of theme foods, and delegate different snacks and drinks to friends.

- Provide plenty of pillows and blankets. If you don't have enough, make sure your friends don't come empty-handed.

Whether the roommate is your partner in crime or not, cleaning up is important. It's your party, your guests, and your room, so take responsibility.

········· YELLOW ● LIGHT ·········

Dorm rooms aren't the right spot for the stereotypical college bash. Alcohol is rarely allowed in campus residence halls, and when a year's worth of housing is on the line, these rules are certainly not worth breaking. Be aware of the rules of alcohol in your residence hall. Some allow it if you're of age, while others vehemently prohibit it.

## Game Night

- Have a game night with three or four board games and a whole floor of friends.

- Have playful snacks, like popcorn and pretzels, and ask friends to chip in extra refreshments.

- Set the scene with rope lighting and a festive play-list, or recruit a musically inclined pal for DJ duty.

### Dorm Dinner Parties

- Give the dining hall a rest and throw a dinner party for your dorm friends.

- If you don't have access to a full kitchen, don't be too proud to let the grocery store lend a hand.

- As long as the dinner is semi-homemade, or at least served on dishes rather than out of plastic containers, your friends will be impressed.

ENTERTAINING

# VIDEO GAMES

## Gaming: the perfect way to unwind after a long day of classes

Video games are as vital as coffee in the lives of many college students. They provide a perfect getaway from the reality of classes, exams, and term papers and are a cheap, convenient form of entertainment.

Whether you consider yourself a "gamer" or not, video games are a great way to socialize with friends in a laid-back setting. Video games have a bit of a stigma, bringing to mind students with bloodshot eyes and faces aglow from the graphics of the game. In reality, kicking back with a round of Guitar Hero is fun and social.

When it comes to video games, the more players, the merrier. Make it a point not to play by yourself. Instead, invite a new friend from across the hall or get together with a group of pals.

### Video Games

- Store your video games in a binder, and put the binder among your textbooks on a bookshelf. This way, others will be less likely to help themselves to your game collection.

- If you're going to sit around playing video games for hours on end (hey, nothing's wrong with that!), consider interactive games like golf and tennis.

- Party-friendly games—namely Guitar Hero and Rock Band—will have fellow students coming from floors away to partake in *American Idol: Dorm Edition*.

### Multiuse Gaming Consoles

- Choosing a video game console is a very personal decision; however, Xboxes make sense for small spaces.

- The Internet accessibility allows users to download TV shows and surf the Web straight from the television set.

- The Xbox also serves as a movie player, playing standard DVD disks.

It doesn't matter if you don't know a joystick from a Wii baton, or Mario Kart from *NASCAR* Kart Racing. The point is to have fun with friends . . . and if a little friendly competition develops, even better.

## *Gaming Controllers*

- Invest in a few extra controllers if you're bringing your gaming system to school to accommodate extra friends (and gaming accidents).

- Opt for wireless controllers if available, because a dorm floor filled with cords can be a little hazardous to even the least accident-prone person.

- Store your controllers in a basket, and keep the cords under control with twist ties.

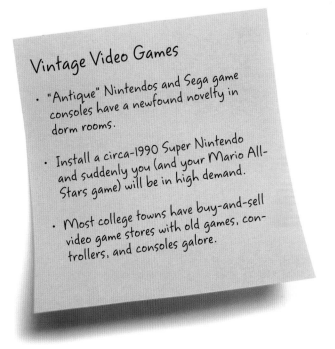

### Vintage Video Games

- "Antique" Nintendos and Sega game consoles have a newfound novelty in dorm rooms.

- Install a circa-1990 Super Nintendo and suddenly you (and your Mario All-Stars game) will be in high demand.

- Most college towns have buy-and-sell video game stores with old games, controllers, and consoles galore.

ENTERTAINING

# KITCHEN STAPLES
## Staying satisfied with a well-stocked kitchen (or cabinet)

At first sight, college cafeterias look like the holy culinary grail: buffets of burgers, fries, pizza, and chicken nuggets; around-the-clock soft-serve; and unlimited chocolate chip cookies just like Mom used to bake.

A few weeks in, the fast-food free-for-all will lose its luster (or some of its appeal, at least), and homemade delicacies will sound better than ever. For those nights when you'd love

nothing more than to head home for an evening of from-scratch home cooking, keep reliable kitchen staples on hand to whip something up yourself.

Depending on your meal plan, the majority of your food will come courtesy of the cafeteria. Although fruits and vegetables are certainly important, remind yourself that produce stays fresh just a few days.

### Produce and Fresh Food

- If the only food you keep around the room is mac 'n' cheese, the only food you'll eat around your room is—you guessed it—mac 'n' cheese.

- Keeping fresh produce accessible will dramatically improve your fruit and veggie consumption. Wouldn't

Mom be proud?

- Apples and oranges stay fresh for a week or so; store them in a big bowl and set them as a centerpiece on your desk.

- Precut carrots, celery, and broccoli make a quick snack.

### Prepackaged Snacks

- A basket filled with pre-packaged snacks makes for a perfect grab-and-go snack on the way to class.

- By "prepackaged snacks," we don't mean Twinkies and potato chips.

- Nutritious food can come in the same shiny packages

as their processed counter-parts. Look for organic or all-natural alternatives to favorite snack foods.

- In addition to the typical healthy fare—granola bars, mini boxes of cereal—you can find everything from cookies to crackers in con-venient single-serving bags.

When you head to the grocery store, look through the canned food aisle for shelf-stable vegetables; they last for months and, with the right recipes, can taste even better than fresh. While you're in the nonperishables, take a peek at the abundance of delicious soups that are filling and fabulously easy to fix.

The sudden abundance of single-serving prepackaged food is geared toward one group of people: college students (*okay*, and small children, but it's not much of a departure if you think about it).

### Cans and Shelf-Stable Foods

- Canned food might not make the most glamorous meals, but it's cheap, convenient, and tasty.

- Keep a few of your favorite soups on hand at all times. With a cup of frozen vegetables and a few whole grain crackers, a canned soup makes a warm, well-rounded meal.

- Cans don't take up valuable refrigerator space and they stay fresh for months.

- Some canned food is high in sodium and sugar to make it tastier; pay attention to the nutrition labels, and be selective.

### Coffee and Caffeinated Drinks

- In college it's often harder to keep up your energy than your grades. Sometimes you don't get enough sleep; sometimes caffeine is *necessary*.

- It isn't healthy to consume *too* many caffeinated products, but a cup of coffee certainly won't hurt.

- Keep an eye on your soda consumption. It's easy to replace your daily water with cans of cola.

- An excess of sugar, chemicals, and caffeine can hurt your academic performance *and* your health.

EATING

# COOKING APPLIANCES
## From prep ware to coffee pots, microwaves to mixing bowls

Most college campuses forbid fancy cooking appliances like hot plates, countertop grills, and toaster ovens. They aren't doing this just to make you go hungry. These contraband appliances violate fire regulations *and* take up a lot of space that your dorm room just doesn't have.

There are a few that you can have, and only a few that you truly need anyway. A microwave, for one, is a must for any college student who hopes to eat. A coffeemaker comes in handy for college students who hope to stay awake, especially through late nights of studying and early mornings of class.

Other cooking basics include measuring cups and spoons. Several kitchen companies make affordable, efficient sets that include everything you could possibly need in a kitchen (if that's what you can call your microwave-topped minifridge).

### Microwaves

- If your dorm room doesn't come with a microwave—some do, some don't—buy one!

- Since your room won't be equipped with an oven or stove top, a microwave is a necessity.

- Use it for everything from making frozen meals to heating up canned soup to reheating last night's dinner (never overlook the possibilities of leftovers).

- Believe it or not, you can come up with elaborate meals with the help of a modern micro.

### Water Purifiers

- The taste of water differs regionally, so the dorm's $H_2O$ won't taste like the stuff from home.

- Give it a week, and if you just can't get used to the taste, invest in a water purifier.

- Water-purifier pitchers

are easy, compact, and efficient. You might even find yourself drinking more water because it's so handy.

- Make sure the purifier you buy fits into your minifridge—oftentimes the shelves are so shallow that you'll have to buy the smallest pitcher.

Even if you aren't whipping up recipes, measuring utensils will keep serving sizes under control.

Water-purifier pitchers and electric teakettles, which are affordable and indescribably useful, bring balance to your caffeine-to-water ratio. Keep the water pitcher filled around-the-clock, and aim to drink a few glasses of water a day. Electric kettles boil water in a flash, perfect for a quick cup of tea. In addition to hot beverages, kettles can be used to fix oatmeal, mac 'n' cheese, and other college staples.

## Cooking Prep Ware

- A quality set of basic cooking prep ware will last you long past college.

- You can buy a starter set with everything you might need, or you can put together your own collection with the essentials.

- Measuring utensils, mixing bowls, and stirring spoons are the pillars of a well-stocked kitchen.

- Even if you don't anticipate doing much cooking, using measuring cups and spoons to dole out servings keeps portions under control—and may help ward off the "freshmen fifteen."

## Coffeemakers

- The quickest way to go into college debt? Pick up a Starbucks-a-day habit.

- Investing in a coffeemaker saves you loads of money *and* allows you to control how much caffeine you consume.

- Five-cup machines are cheap enough to toss after a few years of college. If you go for the full-size coffeemaker, buy something that'll last you through early adulthood.

- If a classic coffeemaker leaves you craving cappuccinos and lattes, consider an espresso machine.

EATING

# COLLEGE MEAL PLANS
## How many meals does it take to earn an A?

Most kids go into college with a three-meals-a-day plan. After all, that's how many meals you eat at home, and isn't a dorm just home away from home? In reality you just won't make it to the cafeteria for each and every meal. Class, friends, and life get in the way of the dining hall's hours. So you thought only retirement communities served dinner at 5 p.m.? Colleges do, too.

If you want to eat meals on your own schedule, cut back your meal plan to two meals a day or even fewer and supplement it with easy in-room meals like cereal, soup, and sandwiches.

Many schools offer plans of ten or twelve meals a week, and unused "points" go toward campus grocers, restaurants, and cafes. Many larger universities have deals with outside vendors,

### Cafeteria Food

- It isn't hard to come up with a nutritious meal at the dining hall. Grab a tray and load up on fresh veggies and fruit.

- Choose a main dish that's packed with protein. Deli sandwiches, grilled

- lean meats, and whole grain pasta—easy on the cheese—are great options.

- The key is *not* to try a little bit of everything. Pick and choose your favorites, and balance comfort foods with healthy staples.

### Dining Hall Takeout

- Most dining halls allow to-go meals, which are useful when you need to eat on the go or scarf food down while studying.

- A slice of pizza might be the easiest thing to grab, but usually the fastest foods are the worst.

- A turkey-on-wheat sandwich or giant chef salad fuels those late nights.

- Moderation is key—a sliver of cheese pizza or one chocolate chip cookie for a late-night snack won't hurt!

which really open up the meal options. Instead of being limited to, say, cafeteria casserole, you can use your points toward a large cheese pizza from your favorite pizza place.

Look into the options your school offers and talk to other students to find out what most people opt to do.

## YELLOW ● LIGHT

Monitor how much you're spending on your meal plan and how many unused meals go to waste each week. This is something that can easily go unnoticed, but makes quite a difference in the long run. Nothing beats the convenience of cafeteria food, but if you aren't getting the most out of your money, an alternative meal option may be your best bet.

## Fast Food

- Sometimes you can't be bothered with the cafeteria; sometimes fast food is a must.

- You can make a fine meal from the drive-through menu if you zoom in on soups, sandwiches, and salads.

- Consider supplementing a taco with a side salad from the cafeteria. Adding a few fresh ingredients can transform lowly fast food.

- Give coffee a break: Make a meal out of a muffin from the corner cafe with a few pieces of fruit.

### "Weighing" Your Options

- If the only cafeteria food that seems edible is from the soft-serve ice-cream machine or home-baked cookie station, rethink your meal plan.

- Before you drop the dorm food altogether, consider the alternatives.

- Can you spice up their sleepy sandwiches with your own condiments? Can you talk to the chefs about adding meal options? Can you get by without a meal plan—or the use of a full kitchen?

# CAFETERIA SHORTCUTS
## Eating your way around, in, and out of the cafeteria

Even if your experience with cooking is limited to watching the Food Network (gotta start somewhere!), you can be a budding chef with a few recipes, a handful of basic ingredients, and a little free time.

The cafeteria isn't *just* filled with the fast-food fantasies of your childhood. The salad bar is stocked with fresh vegetables, the sandwich stand is overflowing with healthy lunch staples,

and the breakfast bar has cereal and fruit for the taking.

Does that mean you should stuff your pockets with cheeseburgers and club sandwiches? Well, no, not unless you don't mind being known as the kid who pockets cafeteria food.

Use take-out containers to your benefit, and load up on vegetables from the salad bar, fruit from the breakfast spread, and bread from the sandwich station. These basic ingredients are

### Precut Produce

- Think of it this way: The cafeteria enables you to eat healthily by cutting the vegetables for you. Isn't that nice of them?

- Baby carrots, celery stalks, and pepper slices are ideal for mindless munching.

- Keep a container of hummus in your fridge, and make a meal out of it. A stack of whole grain crackers snagged from the soup station will take it to the next level.

### Fresh Fruit

- Keep a bowl of fruit on your desk for easy eating. Apples and oranges stay fresh for a few weeks and pack a nutritious punch.

- When they're plentiful, take a handful of grapefruit, kiwi, and stone fruits (peaches,

- plums, apricots), which can be enjoyed at room temperature.

- Every time you eat lunch at the cafeteria, grab an extra container of fruit salad for an afternoon snack.

enough to whip up a simple meal that would make Rachael Ray smile.

Use nesting bowls and brightly colored containers to store your cafeteria contraband. Look for kitchen goods that are microwave safe so you can pop leftovers in the microwave without dirtying more dishes.

## Packaged Dairy Products

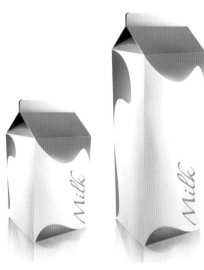

- There's a reason why Mom always told you to drink your milk. The calcium and protein are just as important now as they were when you were five.

- Cereal with milk is a perfect study snack . . . and cookies with milk aren't too shabby either.

- Milk and other dairy products are filled with vitamins and nutrients that aid in keeping your mind in tip-top shape.

- Your body might be done growing, but your brain isn't. Drink milk—and that goes for cow's milk, soy milk, and any other alternatives.

## Snacks

- Stealing snacks from the cafeteria may sound sneaky, but remind yourself that you're paying big bucks for that meal plan.

- Dry foods like peanut butter sandwiches or a bagel and cream cheese are easy to grab on the go.

- Don't miss individually packed snacks like mini cereal boxes, pretzel bags, and little containers of hummus.

- Take advantage of the precut veggies on the salad bar. With a little (or a lot!) of peanut butter, carrots and celery never tasted so good.

EATING

# MAKESHIFT MEALS
## Spur-of-the-moment suppers and last-minute lunches

Elaborate meals are out of the question when you're operating with a microwave and a minifridge, but with a little creativity, you can whip up meals Mom would be proud of . . . or meals she would at least *eat*.

Eating well-rounded meals increases satiety *and* your ability to study. Spur-of-the-moment meals call for great basics and good intentions; you don't have to spend a fortune to make something that's nutritious and delicious. Try to taste at least three different food groups at a time. If you're going to grab a peanut butter sandwich, add slices of banana. If you're craving cheese and crackers, top it with a few slivers of avocado.

Buy basics that won't go bad after a few days. Canned tomato soup can be combined with dried whole grain

### Soup

- College sparks spur-of-the-moment comfort-food cravings, and soup is a healthful and hearty way to indulge in homey cooking.

- Doctor up a can of soup with vegetables, legumes, or prepared chicken, or snag a insulated coffee cup full of soup from the cafeteria.

- A thick slice of whole grain bread is the perfect accompaniment to soup. Grains are packed with protein and fiber—neither of which is abundant in a pizza-dependant diet.

### Crudités

- A well-rounded snack plate can serve you well as a meal if you dabble in a few different food groups.

- A plate of vegetables with pita bread (or crackers or bread) and a scoop of hummus is nutritious and pretty delicious, too.

- Crudités with dip is the perfect college meal, because you can nibble while you study and sneak in several servings of vegetables.

noodles to make a quick pasta dish. A splash of soy sauce—which lasts for months and makes anything more delectable—can turn brown rice and frozen vegetables into a faux stir-fry.

## Sandwiches

- In college, a sandwich is a food group in itself. Using staples from the cafeteria and a few minifridge ingredients, a sandwich works any time of day.

- Skip the white bread, which has the nutritional value of a slice of cake, and use whole grain bread.

- Deli meat, cheese, and mustard make a stick-to-your-ribs sandwich. Extra points (and extra nutrients!) for incorporating vegetables.

## Salads

- Salads are nutritious and necessary, but aren't easy to whip together from a minifridge.

- Salad components take up a lot of space and only stay fresh for a few days.

- Take advantage of the salad bar every time you hit the cafeteria.

- Even if you're just nibbling on a side salad, every vegetable is chock-full of vitamins that you just can't get from midnight pizza deliveries.

EATING

# SMART SNACKS
## Even college students need after-school snacks

When hunger strikes a few hours before mealtime, stop yourself before reaching for the vending machine. Smart snacks keep you going through the day. Silly snacks, like cookies, chips, and other nutritionless goodies, are completely counterproductive, zapping energy instead of boosting it.

Natural whole foods, like fruit, vegetables, and nuts, make superior snacks filled with good things *and* great taste.

Gnawing on raw celery isn't necessary; trail mixes, yummy dips, and nutty spreads can make measly veggies delectable.

Instead of snacking the afternoon away, think in terms of minimeals. In addition to your three-squares-a-day, make mid-afternoon hunger an excuse to sneak in some food groups you may have neglected earlier in the day. This means choosing string cheese over Cheetos, fresh apples over apple

### Trail Mix

- Buy a big container of trail mix or stock up on a bag at your local grocer's bulk bins.

- Make your own with a combination of raw nuts, dried fruit, seeds—and chocolate if you're feeling indulgent.

- When nibbling on nuts, keep an eye on how many you consume. They're full of nutrients, but they aren't a light snack.

- For a little variety, buy nut-and-fruit bars, which pack all of the goodness of trail mix into a handy bar.

### Nut Butters

- A PB&J may have been a lunchbox favorite back in elementary school, but these days it makes a pretty wonderful snack, too.

- Forgo traditional jam in favor of thinly sliced bananas, smashed berries, or shredded carrots.

- If you love peanut butter, try other nut butters made from almonds, cashews, or hazelnuts.

- Nut butters are a tasty addition to fresh fruit and vegetables.

strudel Pop-Tarts, and peanut butter and jelly on whole grain bread over chocolate peanut butter cups.

## *Fresh Fruit*

- The perfect snack is simple and balanced; fruit alone doesn't suffice.

- Slice an apple and add a slice of string cheese for a succulent, protein-packed snack.

- Grapes are great with sharp cheddar, pineapple works wonders on top of Greek yogurt, and oranges are delicious with a handful of almonds.

## *Raw Vegetables*

- You get it: Vegetables are important. But we get it: Choosing a salad over your cafeteria's signature double cheeseburger just isn't going to happen.

- Instead of depriving yourself, simply make a point to snack on virtuous veggies.

- With yummy dips, the lowly baby carrot becomes a delicious vehicle for shoveling salsa, guacamole, and hummus into your mouth.

EATING

# TELEVISION

## Must-see TV, season-premiere parties, and show marathons

Sometimes you just have to kick back and watch TV. Even if you aren't a self-proclaimed coach potato, a really good (or sometimes really, really bad) television show can be the perfect way to relax.

You're a big kid now, so you could skip class and watch TV all day. Or you could be an upstanding college student and only tune in when you have nothing else to do (and we mean nothing else!). Watch TV with a purpose. If a favorite TV show is on, flip it on. If an exciting new movie just debuted on DVD, rent it. But if you find yourself staring at the tube, clicker in hand, eyes glazed over, go out and do something.

Remember that television will be a constant in your life; college will not. Take advantage of the campus television stations, your roommate's DVR, and that techie student's dish.

### DVD Players

- A no-frills DVD player is all you need to get through a year in the dorm. If it plays movies, it's perfect.

- If you don't already have a TV for your room, consider buying a set with a built-in DVD player.

- Don't split the cost of a DVD player with a roommate, because only one of you will keep it at the end of the year.

- Depending on your school's cable package, you might have a plethora of movie channels and won't even need a DVD player.

### DVR

- With classes, test reviews, and cram sessions, your schedule will be unpredictable at best.

- A DVR ensures that you won't get behind with your favorite TV shows when you're getting ahead at school.

- If you're fanatical about *Grey's Anatomy* but one of your club meetings falls on the same night it airs, a DVR might be worth it.

- If you're an occasional TV watcher who's just as content catching *Law & Order* episodes as the national news, save your cash.

But also take advantage of the opportunities that four years at college afford you.

You don't have the space for an in-room theater, and you don't need a wide-screen TV. It isn't worth the extra cash, especially when you could use the extra desk space for valuable things like . . . textbooks. If you can't install a flat-screen on the wall, keep the TV at a spot where both you and your roommate can see. Storing it on top of a dresser is much less distracting than keeping it on your desk.

## *Dish*

- There's always a kid who hooks his TV up with every high-tech appliance on the market. You don't have to be that kid.

- Some schools throw in satellite program fees with the dorm package; most don't.

- So should you buy your own? Maybe. If you love TV and can't bear the thought of missing a few of your favorites, investing in a satellite program might be worth it to you.

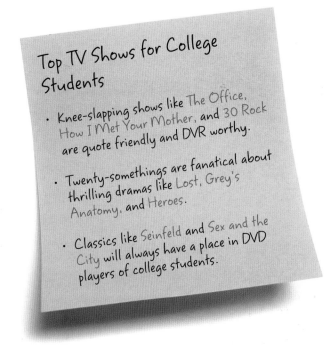

**Top TV Shows for College Students**

- Knee-slapping shows like The Office, How I Met Your Mother, and 30 Rock are quote friendly and DVR worthy.

- Twenty-somethings are fanatical about thrilling dramas like Lost, Grey's Anatomy, and Heroes.

- Classics like Seinfeld and Sex and the City will always have a place in DVD players of college students.

# MOVIES
## A little entertainment is good for the mind

Kicking back with a good movie is like recharging with a nap—a lovely break from reality and a wonderful refresher. Although watching a movie might not seem like a big priority in the midst of a long school day, taking an hour or two to watch a little fluff can actually make you more productive in the long run.

If friends and roommates are in and out all day, a laptop might provide the best movie experience. Coupled with a powerful pair of headphones (surround sound, anyone?) and a stack of pillows, you can create your own little theater experience.

Instead of taking up loads of shelf space, keep your DVDs organized in a neat binder. An added bonus, other than saving serious storage space, is that friends will be far less likely

### Movie Collection

- Don't bring your entire collection of DVDs, but do bring a diverse selection of favorites.

- Movies are a huge conversation starter, and they add a nice diversity to your shelves filled with textbooks.

- Store movie disks alphabetically in a binder, or display a comprehensive DVD collection on a spare bookshelf.

- Friends will inevitably borrow movies here and there, so scrawl initials on each disk to remind others where unclaimed DVDs belong.

### Renting Movies

- Renting movies is *always* a better option than buying; unless it's a movie you'll watch time and time again, renting saves space *and* money.

- If you haven't already, sign up at a local movie rental store so you can rent movies whenever you want.

- Movie stores occasionally honor student discounts and offer deals throughout the year.

- Movie vending machines, like Redbox, charge as little as a dollar per day for a DVD rental.

to borrow movies when they're hidden this way.

Unless you're a movie connoisseur, rent or borrow movies instead of buying them. Not only is it more economical, but you'll save loads of shelf space. Sign up for Netflix, which saves trips to and from the movie store and all but eliminates late fees. Find out if your campus has a Redbox vending kiosk, which charges a dollar a night for movie rentals.

## Seeing Movies

- Since seeing a movie at the theater costs the same price as a week's worth of ramen, keep track of these outings.

- Ask around about movie theaters that offer discounts for students who have their ID on hand.

- Discounts on matinees—in the afternoon or early in the morning—are often as much as half the regular price.

### Best College Movies

- Animal House is the most classic college movie, hands down, but there are tons of other hilariously collegiate flicks.

- Old School and Van Wilder will make you want to stay an undergrad forever, while Glory Daze and PCU will make you excited for the archetypal college experience.

- Dead Man on Campus and Urban Legend are terribly fun but will make you a little fearful of your roommates.

# MUSIC
## Turn up the tunes and chill out

Music is indispensable. It aids relaxation, improves concentration, and makes studying for hours on end a whole lot more enjoyable.

Boom boxes—a major mainstay in college dorms of the '80s—are a thing of the past; these days all you really need to set the mood is a pair of speakers with an iPod-friendly jack. Docks are convenient because they allow you to charge your player while streaming music. Many come with a remote control for seamless DJing.

Fill your iPod with music for every occasion. Laid-back tunes are perfect for studying, but when it comes to unwinding, set the scene with a fun mix of oldies and little-known tunes.

Utilize computer programs like iTunes Genius to mix playlists to suit your taste, and then stream them from your computer.

### Mobile Music Players

- An MP3 player will easily be the electronic toy you use most during your college years.

- The compact music player will entertain you to and from class, aid in concentration while studying, and liven up your room when you're just hanging out.

- College towns are a gold mine for cool up-and-coming bands. Familiarize yourself with local bands and small music haunts.

### iPod Speakers

- You can find speakers for less than $20 at electronic stores, and they can turn your dorm room into a dance party.

- Speakers with audio jacks can work for laptops and pocket music players.

- Eliminate cluttered cords and buy wireless speakers, which can be placed all around the room.

- If you have the desktop space, speaker docks are great because they charge the battery as they play tunes.

Many speakers for MP3 players fit laptop jacks, too, allowing you to rig a surround-sound system in your room.

Storing your music digitally saves tons of room, but salvage some of the jewel cases to use as small picture frames. Cut magazine images or music posters to fit, and attach them to the wall in a grid.

**RED●LIGHT**

Don't even think about filling your iPod with illegally downloaded tunes. Many schools block illegal download Web sites, and others keep a *very* close eye on them. Illegally downloading music (and movies) is an easy way to find yourself in the midst of a lawsuit. If you love music, buy it—for your sake and the sake of your favorite bands.

## Records

- If you love classic oldies, an antique record player is a great addition to a dorm room.

- Classic tunes are universally adored, and a stack of records will entertain friends unlike an ordinary CD collection.

- Knowing how to spin a record takes little skill but will amaze even your impossible-to-impress friend.

## Stereos

- Unless you still frequently spin your favorite CDs, a stereo isn't a must-have.

- A good laptop with decent speakers will stand in for a stereo, streaming your favorite music.

- Old-school boom boxes and antique record players add a nice style spin to a room.

# BOOKS

Books aren't just for reading; they can be decorated—and used for decorating!—too

Amid stacks of textbooks, you have piles of novels, paperbacks, and "just for fun" biographies. With a workload as heavy as all those books, they'll be doing far more sitting than you'll be reading. Since they're going to continue taking up space, you might as well make them part of your decor.

Even if books seem like the bane of your existence—"Read ten chapters by Monday!"—they're as indispensable for learning in school as they are for bringing style to your room. Books add color to your shelves and collegiate elegance to your decor.

Stylize your bookshelves with knickknacks and interesting bookends. Break up books with personal items like travel

### Book Decor

- Make books part of your desktop decor by color coding them according to the shade of the spine.

- Stacked horizontally, books can act as a "stand" for artfully arranged knickknacks.

- Set bursts of books around your room, holding them up—and making them look impossibly artsy—with cool bookends or knickknacks.

### Book Nightstand

- Do you collect thick stylish-spined books? Use them as a makeshift nightstand.

- Stack wide books up horizontally from the floor, top them with a plate of glass, and call it a nightstand.

- Scavenge around a used bookstore for thick coffee table books with old-fashioned charm.

- Any sheet of glass will work, but frosted glass looks especially great.

souvenirs, mismatched picture frames, or colorful glass jars filled with office supplies.

Cover books with packing paper and slap on labels to make them uniform; this protects their original covers and gives your bookshelf continuity. Removing jackets from hardcover books shows off a cool vintage look while at the same time ensures the jackets won't rip.

Store books and magazines on wall racks like they have in a doctor's office, or stack them around the room and use these as surface spaces.

## GREEN ● LIGHT

When it comes time to buy textbooks, opt for used books. Not only are they cheaper, but they're much greener— less paper, less consumption. At the end of the summer, sell the textbooks back to the campus bookstore or donate them to the university.

### *Reading for Pleasure*

- Make books part of your routine—and not just the mandatory textbooks. Picking up a novel now and then will give you a short reprieve from reality.

- An abundance of academic books look boring on a bookshelf; mix it up with coffee table tomes and interesting best sellers.

- Make it a point to read something completely different than what you spend your days studying. If you're a science major, indulge in a little Shakespeare now and then.

### Dealing with Textbooks

- While it's easy to order textbooks from the campus bookstore, off-price stores— both off-campus and online—sell the very same textbooks for a fraction of the price.

- There are plenty of Web sites that offer used books in top condition for a fraction of the price. You can use these same sites to resell books as well.

- Some professors list far more recommended textbooks than they actually require. Buy books a few days in to decide which will actually be used.

127

# LOUNGING
## Finding comfort in a closet-size room

As great as the library is, sometimes all you want to do is lounge. Make your dorm room as relaxing as possible with pillows, blankets, and other things that make you feel warm and fuzzy inside and out.

It's tough to chill out in the same room you study, sleep, and spend time stressing out about your next term paper. There's no good way to keep your school space separate from your unwinding space—your bed undoubtedly serves both purposes—so carefully schedule separate time to do both.

Designate when you need to work and when you can relax; don't watch TV while writing a paper or Facebook with friends while studying for a test. Work hard, but give yourself a breather or you'll burn out—and *fast*.

Extra blankets and adequate pillows are a must for bringing

### Floor Pillows

- Make a dorm-room floor look like a luxurious couch . . . almost.

- Floor pillows are a worth-while way to turn your dorm room into a cozy lounge.

- Load up on a handful of floor pillows in different colors, sizes, and patterns to create a denlike atmosphere.

- Look for floor pillows with removable covers. You can change the look by switching the case, and it makes for easy cleaning.

### Extra Blankets and Pillows

- No need to splurge on fancy covers. For extra blankets and pillows, anything will do.

- Vintage afghans, home-made quilts, and remnants of flannel or fleece all bring a little luxury to a small room.

- Store blankets in an old-fashioned trunk, or keep a stack on the edge of your bed.

- Blankets can also be tossed up on a closet's top shelf or rolled up and stuffed onto a shelf.

comfort to a dorm room. Papasan cushions—the coverings for circle chairs—are perfect as floor pillows. Poufs are like cushioned ottomans that can be used for cozy seating or cool surface space.

Once you cozy up into pillows, blankets, and cushions, set the scene with music. Nothing is as therapeutic as blasting a playlist that makes you smile.

## Loungers and Sleeping Bags

- Don't have room for a couch? Turn your floor into a sofa with a lounger or sleeping bag.

- Sleeping bags, either from the kids' department or camping-supply stores, can be easily stashed away.

- Loungers are like one-person futons—more compact, but just as cozy.

### Lounging Outside Your Room

- Don't feel chained to your desk. On a pretty day, grab a blanket and a book and head to the quad for some fresh air.

- Closing your computer for an hour or two will give you a fresh perspective and a renewed sense of focus.

- Designate a blanket for outdoors. For extra comfort, buy a roll-up cot or patio lounge-chair cushion.

# NAP ESSENTIALS
## Making time for shut-eye in an overstuffed schedule

Sometimes you'll catch ten hours of sleep; sometimes you'll catch two. For those days when a cup of coffee (or five!) just won't cut it, learning how to nap efficiently with quiet-time essentials will boost your productivity—and your sanity.

Whether you're trying to study during your roommate's marathon of *Star Trek* or some neighbors are throwing a raging midnight dance party, catching sorely needed beauty sleep requires a brigade of nap inducers.

A nice pair of noise-canceling headphones will be music to your ears, and a sleep mask can hide roommate high jinks and friendly drop-ins when you want nothing else than to grab some shut-eye.

It's been said that napping boosts memory and improves concentration, so squeezing in a nap right before a cram

### Headphones

- Buy headphones that are comfy enough to sleep in—sometimes you're going to need 'em.

- Earbuds that squeeze inside of your ear are more com-

fortable than buds that rest on the exterior.

- Listen to music at a very low volume or play nature sounds or white noises to lull you to sleep.

### Sleep Masks

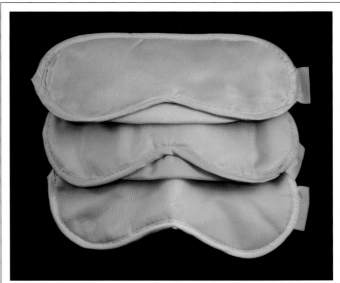

- A sleep mask allows you to snooze in the middle of the day.

- For as little as five bucks, a sleep mask can block outside light. Even better, it serves as a Do Not Disturb sign, signaling to room-

mates and friends that you're trying to sleep.

- A silk mask is soft on your eyes and looks very Holly Golightly. Keep it glam by washing it regularly—smudges of eye makeup are anything but elegant.

session might be more beneficial than a post-exam slumber.

Twenty to forty minutes is the ideal amount of time for a midday sleep, so you can sneak in a quick nap between classes, before dinner, or even right before a big night out on the town.

## Earplugs

- A set of earplugs, which cost pennies, are priceless.

- Look for earplugs made of silicone or foam that conform to your ear.

- Earplugs don't look particularly cool, but skin-colored plugs are inconspicuous—and lifesaving.

## Making a Habit of Napping

- Don't use naps as an excuse not to get enough sleep during the night.

- If you're sleepy in the afternoon, a nap's okay, but don't go to bed as the sun comes up because you're counting on a nap.

- Make sure to limit your nap time. Don't sleep all afternoon—this will hinder a good night's sleep.

# TOILETRIES

From shampoo to soap, make the most of the dorm shower with top-notch toiletries

Going off to college means leaving behind the luxury of a well-stocked bathroom. Make the most of the shower stall with top-notch toiletries that will remind you of the scents and smells of home.

Stock up on bath supplies; buy oversize bottles and multiples of everything so you don't have to worry about running out of soap right before a big date.

Look for extra-large bottles of shampoo, conditioner, and body wash. Store the oversize containers in your closet and cart smaller, refillable plastic bottles to the shower each day.

Keep all of your bathroom necessities in coordinated totes and pouches, and store toiletries like cotton balls, Q-tips, and

## Shampoo

- Buy shampoo in bulk and you'll never have to worry about running out.

- If you keep your shampoo in the shower, don't splurge on the fancy stuff—your roommates will undoubt-edly help themselves to your salon-quality hair stuff.

- If you have a short hair-cut or low-maintenance do, choose a shampoo-conditioner combination to cut down on bottles.

## Soap

- When it comes to dorm bathrooms, a bottle of body wash is a much better option than a bar of soap.

- It's easier to lug from dorm room to bathroom, and you don't have to worry about dropping the bar on the grimy shower floor.

- If you use a washcloth or loofah, make sure to wring it out and hang it up to avoid mildew.

makeup pads in tidy glass jars, which can be found at supply stores for a few bucks apiece.

With classic glass bottles and presentation-worthy containers, toiletries can double as shelf decorations. Stack sugar bowls, creamer dishes, and tiny teacups on a platter, and use the small compartments to stow makeup brushes, cotton balls, and travel-size products.

## MAKE IT EASY

Moving to college is a great time to go through your toiletries with a fine-tooth comb. Do you *really* need three kinds of shampoo and five different hair brushes? Simplify your bathroom necessities to the bare essentials.

### Toothbrush

- Store your toothbrush in a pretty juice glass or frosted jar on your desk, along with your makeup brushes and tools.

- Suction toothbrush holders can be pressed on a bathroom mirror or medicine cabinet.

- Look for toothbrushes in bright colors that will blend into your room's decor—and don't forget to buy a new toothbrush every three to four months!

### Displaying Toiletries

- Nice bottles make even the simplest product look fancy. Transfer dime-store shampoo and soap into uniform plastic bottles.

- Slap on cute labels, either over the existing labels or onto the refurbished glass jars.

- Decorative trays can corral a desktop full of products in the prettiest way. Little containers and beauty supplies suddenly look stylish when displayed on a vintage tray.

# TOWELS

## Dry off with bath linens that double as decoration

Something you've never given a second thought to before is suddenly on display for all to see. Faded, fraying bath towels may have worked at home, but when you're wandering the halls covered only in a bath towel, a new, larger variety is preferable.

Since you won't have a linen closet to store your towels, choose shades that match your overall color scheme. As long as they coordinate, towels can double as room decor.

Come to school with at least five new towels to allow you to start each week with a fresh one. Bath towels should be changed out every few days—every week at *least*—so just a few towels should suffice if you do laundry with any sort of regularity. If you only do laundry every few weeks, buy an extra or two.

### Bath Towels

- Buy bright colors and incorporate them into your decor by storing them in stylish stacks.

- Roll towels crosswise, then store them in a pretty basket with bath products.

- Classic bath towels are 27 x 52 inches; oversize bath towels, commonly referred to as bath sheets, are a cozy 35 x 60 inches.

- For dorm bathrooms, bath sheets allow for speedy dry-offs inside the tiny shower stall and allow extra coverage to and from the bathroom.

### Beach Towels

- Similar to bath sheets, beach towels are bigger, sturdier, and, oftentimes, brighter.

- Because beach towels can be found as big as 40 x 70 inches, they're big enough for wrapping up with and roaming the halls in.

- Don't reuse ages-old beach towels; invest in a stack of new ones. At the end of the summer, they'll be abundant and on sale.

Instead of buying five towels in the same color, buy two patterned towels and three or four in coordinating colors. Fold clean bath towels in a neat pile, or roll the towels and cinch them with contrasting ribbon.

Tossing a towel on the back of your chair (or worse, the floor!) will attract mildew in an instant. If you don't have a built-in towel rack in your room, an over-the-door rack can hang a towel *and* hold tomorrow's outfit on a hanger.

## Hair Towels

- Hair-turban towels are made of microfiber fabric that dries hair in half the time.

- For hair that's really long and really thick, a hair towel might be a good addition to your bath accessories.

- Not only can they cut down on styling time, they can also eliminate going to bed with sopping wet hair at 2 a.m.

- Is your hair low maintenance as it is? Skip this extra towel.

## Washing Bath Towels

- Switch out clean bath towels every few days. Hard to keep track? If they don't smell fresh, they probably aren't.

- When washing, use dryer sheets instead of fabric softener, which actually stiffens towels and reduces absorbency.

- Because most dorm dryers are exceedingly hot, remove towels a few minutes before the time runs out to stave off shrinkage.

- Fold them immediately to reduce wrinkles.

# SHOWER ATTIRE
## What to wear to and from the bathroom

Living in a dorm often means showering down the hall. Unless you're comfortable passing classmates, boyfriends, and parents wearing little more than an unraveling terry cloth bath towel, stock up on shower attire.

It isn't a concept that serves much purpose before college, but bath wear—a wardrobe for wearing to and from the bathroom—makes community showering far more enjoyable.

Once you dry off, cover up in an oversize bathrobe. Terry cloth is comfortable and wicks away moisture, so you'll continue to dry off as you make your way from the bathroom back to your room.

Another option? Bath wraps. Just like they sound, bath wraps look like towels but stay in place with the help of Velcro or button closures. Many come trimmed in ribbons or

### Bathrobes

- Choose a bathrobe that's fancy enough to roam the halls in, but comfy enough to wear on a daily basis.

- Look for a bathrobe that's not too short—at least 35 inches for girls, 45 inches for guys.

- Stick with materials that wick away moisture: plush terry cloth for the cooler months, light cotton during the warmer months.

### Shower Shoes

- Good ol' rubber flip-flops are pretty great shower shoes. The simplicity and comfort are hard to beat.

- Sandals with a bit of a platform might come in handy for showers that don't drain as well as they should.

- Nonskid soles are great for slippery showers.

136

adorned in monograms; others come in coordinating colors with sets of towels.

If you're going to be sharing a shower space with the opposite sex, wearing a bathrobe to and from the shower might be preferable. Wearing actual clothing to the shower is quite an inconvenience for even the most modest among us. If you don't feel comfortable in a bath wrap or robe, a T-shirt and shorts aren't too much of a hassle.

## Towel Wraps

- Guys and girls alike will find towel wraps indispensable. They're cooler than robes, but infinitely more convenient than wrapping up in a bath towel.

- Make your own with a strip of sew-on Velcro and a terry cloth towel.

- Girls should choose larger towels (cozy 35 x 60 inches), while guys can opt for a shorter 27 x 52 length.

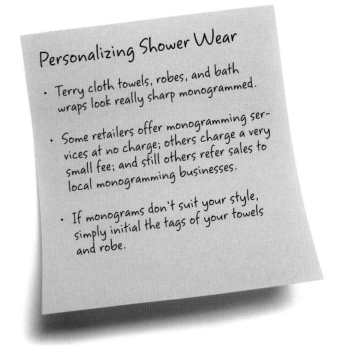

Personalizing Shower Wear

- Terry cloth towels, robes, and bath wraps look really sharp monogrammed.

- Some retailers offer monogramming services at no charge; others charge a very small fee; and still others refer sales to local monogramming businesses.

- If monograms don't suit your style, simply initial the tags of your towels and robe.

# CADDIES
## Store bath supplies in style

Lugging bottles of shampoo, conditioner, body wash, and shaving cream from room to shower and back again without a caddy makes as much sense as leaving your backpack at home while you go from class to class.

Bath caddies make dorm showering—and storage—a cinch. There are a few bath caddies to choose from, depending on your personal preference. From plastic caddies to nylon totes, aeration and style are key.

Plastic caddies with retractable handles make for easy lugging and even easier storage—the handle doubles as a hook for hanging. If you use a lot of products, opt for a vinyl or nylon tote. Plastic caddies can be unwieldy, resulting in tipping shampoos and soap spills. The last thing you want is an overturned caddy, which runs the risk of contaminating your

### Bath Totes

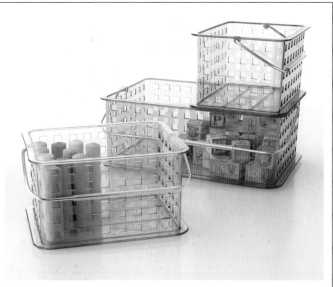

- Stock bath totes with the bare necessities: shampoo, body wash, and conditioner.

- Toss a bottle of lotion in there, too. Moisturizing your bod in a towel in front of a roommate will prove impossible while trying to maintain modesty.

- Postshower, hang the tote up to dry alongside your towel and robe to avoid mildew.

### In-Shower Caddies

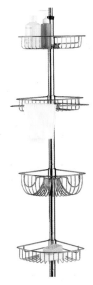

- If you have your own bathroom or share one within your suite, ditch the bath tote and invest in a shower shelf.

- Tension shelves fit right in a shower corner and can accommodate up to four tiers of surface space.

- Another option is a space-saving caddy that fits directly over a showerhead.

toothbrush on the dorm-shower floor.

Can't find a tote intended for bath use? Beach bags have the ventilation and come in bright colors and fun patterns.

A sleek metal wire basket is a timeless option that can be repurposed postdorm as a kitchen carryall. Silverware caddies—especially retro diner ones meant to hold mustard and ketchup—make unique bath totes. However, while this is a chic option, there's nothing stylish about rust, so make sure you keep it out of the shower stall.

## MAKE IT EASY

Look around for household supplies you could use as a shower tote. Cleaning-supply caddies are sturdier than those intended for bath use. If you use a lot of products, check out a home-improvement department where you can find cleaning-supply caddies in nice colors and often with a cheaper price tag.

## Waterproof Totes

- Not just any tote will work. To avoid mildew and messes, look for bags with ventilation and breathable holes.

- Vinyl or nylon totes can stash tons of products, while plastic baskets are better suited for a handful of small bottles.

- Whatever you do, dry off your bath products before you store them in your room, or they'll mildew enough to make a mom cringe.

### Buying Bath Products in Bulk

- Stock up on often-used bath products like shampoo and soap. Not only will it save you some cash, it will help you avoid some errands (a huge plus if you can't have a car on campus!).

- Look for liter-size shampoo, like the pump bottles hairdressers use, and buy the largest body wash you can find.

- Instead of lugging a few pounds' worth of bath products to the shower, just fill up smaller bottles.

# BATH STORAGE
## Storing your bath stuff with style

At home you have a whole bathroom to store your shower goods. At the dorm, you pretty much have . . . a dorm room. Unless you're okay stashing bottles of shampoo alongside stacks of textbooks on your shelves, stylish bath storage is in order.

Bath stuff needs proper storage and a place to dry. Keeping shampoo and soap on your desktop will put a damper on the decor scheme—and dampen your desktop to boot. Baskets, medicine cabinets, and towel racks can stash stuff in a stylish way.

If your room doesn't come with a towel rack or you're not allowed to mount anything on the wall, consider an over-the-door rack or wall hooks. A row of three or four hooks makes hanging towels look stylish, especially if the bath

### Towel Racks

- A towel rack is a necessity to keep your towels off the floor and in fighting shape.

- If the dorm doesn't come with built-in racks, try an over-the-door hook-on stand.

- Another option? Reserve part of your closet's clothing rack for hanging towels.

- Wall hooks hold towels like a charm, but because towels don't dry as evenly when hung on a hook, they're more prone to mildewing.

### Medicine Cabinets

- If you don't have a medicine cabinet, designate one of your desk drawers for bath storage. Line it with cork, which will soak up any shower condensation and prevent warping.

- Use an over-the-door caddy to stash your bath stuff.

- Set aside a few cubbies for shower products, and use the rest for clothes and shoes.

- Mount a medicine cabinet, or simply lean a cool vintage variety on your dresser top—no tools required!

linens coordinate with your bed linens.

Vintage-style apothecary jars conquer little bath products, like clean washcloths, small makeup pads, and tiny cotton balls.

## *Stacking Baskets*

- Stacking baskets store towels and bath goods in one spot.

- Buy plastic containers with slots that allow for draining, or get pretty bins lined with fabric for easy laundering.

- Buy bath storage in fun colors so you don't have to worry about stashing it under your bed.

- Think of storage as an additional design element to your dorm room—even when it comes to something as simple as shampoo.

### Turning Shower Storage into Decor

- If you aren't in a community bathroom, consider the possibilities: Rugs, shower curtains, window curtains, towels, even bathrobes can infuse color and style into an itty-bitty bathroom.

- Always keep your bathroom rack filled with bright, fluffy towels. If you have extra towels on hand, roll them horizontally and stash them in an oversize basket

- If you have your own sink, keep your toiletries and shower accessories organized in little dishes and jars.

141

# BATH ACCESSORIES
## Bath extras to make humble dorm showers better

Your dorm shower won't be the lavish bath experience of your dreams. In fact, you might feel dirtier after spending some quality time in the dingy stall than before you entered. But never mind—a humble shower doesn't mean you can't improve the experience with a few luxurious bath accessories.

If you have your own bathroom—lucky you!—swapping the showerhead can take the water level from sprinkle to downpour, greatly improving your overall shower experience. Consider coordinating the rug and shower curtain with your bath linens, and add nice lotion and soap dispensers around the sink.

In suite-style bathrooms, cool rugs, fun shower curtains, and an in-bathroom iPod dock can make all the difference. Talk to roommates to see who's willing to chip in and help.

### Showerheads

- Clean a shabby showerhead with vinegar for a shine so sparkling it'll look brand-new.

- Store your loofah around the base of your showerhead. Not only is it in a convenient spot, it'll add a serious punch of color to your shower.

- Want to replace the school's showerhead? Don't drop a fortune for a new one; upscale fixtures can be found for well under $50. Just be sure to hold onto the old one for when you move out!

### Shower Radios

- Shower radios can really set the scene in a shabby dorm shower.

- Be mindful of fellow showerers, and don't blast music too loud.

- An in-shower clock radio can blast tunes *and* keep a clock in close view.

If you use a community bathroom, make the most of it with a shower radio, fully stocked bath caddy, and the best shower shoes you can find.

## Personal Care

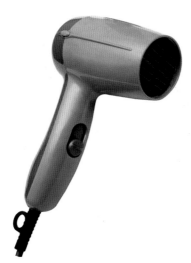

- If you let your hair air dry most days, stick with a travel-size blow dryer.

- To minimize appliances, look for a combination curling iron/straightening iron.

- Store hair appliances and razors in a decorative vase (weigh the bottom down with some glass marbles).

## Shower Caps

- Let's face it: Shower caps don't have a glamorous reputation. In fact they're downright dorky.

- But when you *need* a shower —and fast!—slip on a shower cap, and you'll be out the door in minutes.

- Buy a box of disposable caps, and throw one on right before jumping in the shower.

- Or buy a cute printed cap made from a thicker plastic that can be reused again and again.

# HANGERS

## Big wardrobe, small closet? Make hangers work for you

Having a closet in college is an occasional, though not impossible, luxury. It isn't unheard of to have a nice-size closet, and some residence halls even tout walk-ins—but don't get your hopes up.

No matter how big or small your closet is, it won't be large enough to accommodate your entire wardrobe. The key to making the most of what you get is with clever hanging techniques. Think of it this way: Your wardrobe is only as great as your hanger collection. A rack full of mismatched hangers won't suffice; a great selection of hangers can be used to color code, organize outfits, and keep pants in neat and pressed condition.

Skip the wire hangers, which turn into a tangled mess in an instant. Colorful plastic tubular hangers are sturdy enough

### Closet Organization

- The easiest way to organize a tiny closet is to make use of color, both for the hangers and the clothes.

- Buy several sets of different colored hangers and "color code" your clothes.

- For example, use green for casual, blue for dressy, white for business.

- Take it a step further and organize your clothes by color, season, or level of dressiness.

### Pants Hangers

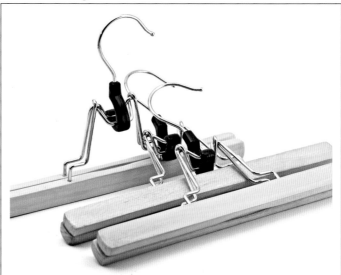

- Dress pants and skirts should be pressed and hung up to take the hassle out of dressing up.

- To make the most of your closet space, toss jackets over your pants hangers.

- As long as you know what's in your closet, doubling your clothes up on hangers doubles your closet space.

- Unless you're really particular about your clothes, fold your jeans and casual bottoms.

to accommodate jackets, but lightweight enough for T-shirts and sweaters. Notched hangers keep sleeveless tops and dresses snugly in place, and no-skid stickers serve the same purpose. Wooden hangers are a nice addition, but they cost quite a bit and take up more space than their plastic counterparts. Save the fancy cedar-closet trimmings for your first apartment.

Unless half of your wardrobe is dress pants, don't worry about specific pants hangers—just pick up a few accessory clips to add to your existing hangers.

## Connectible Hangers

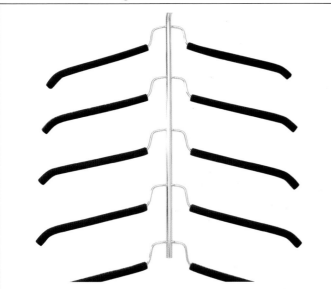

- Also known as wardrobe "trees," connectible hangers connect at the base, creating a "cascading" effect.

- They don't just look pretty, these useful hangers allow numerous pieces of clothing to take up the same amount of space as one.

- Consolidate your closet with a few sets of connectible hangers and combine similar genres of clothing: T-shirts on one hanger, jackets on another.

## Swing-Arm Tiered Hangers

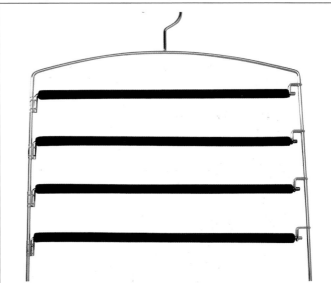

- Tiered hangers boast four or five rows that swing in and out, making retrieving clothing effortless.

- When changing clothes, use a swing-arm hanger to place things that don't need to go straight to the hamper.

- Tiered hangers can also hold blankets, bath towels, and extra sets of sheets.

# SPACE SAVERS

## Even the smallest space has huge storage potential

A closet doubler is a rack that drops down from the existing rack, creating a second tier of storage. This doesn't work in armoires, but the adjustability makes it ideal for closets of all shapes and sizes. This works best for wardrobes filled with tops and short bottoms; dresses and longer skirts won't accommodate a second rack.

Tension rods are similar to closet doublers in that they add an additional clothing rack to the existing closet. With the tension-mounting mechanism, this rod can be placed anywhere—not just below the existing rack, but also above or behind. Most can be adjusted to fit between three to seven feet, and hold up to fifty pounds.

Only certain varieties can handle the weight of clothes, so permanently installing a second closet rod might be your

### Closet Rods

- Use a tension rod as a secondary clothing rack, either by placing it below or behind the original.

- Mounting a tension rod doesn't require tools. Tighten in place with a little elbow grease and a lot of persistence.

- These can hold only up to 50 pounds—and even that is pushing it—so store lightweight clothes on this rod.

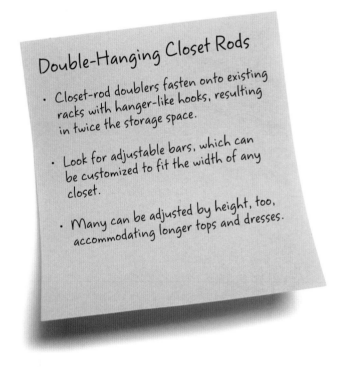

**Double-Hanging Closet Rods**

- Closet-rod doublers fasten onto existing racks with hanger-like hooks, resulting in twice the storage space.

- Look for adjustable bars, which can be customized to fit the width of any closet.

- Many can be adjusted by height, too, accommodating longer tops and dresses.

best bet. They're not expensive, and they're easy to install with screws; just be sure to measure the width of your closet before buying anything and to check that permanent fixtures are not against dorm regulations.

Garment bags are made to ease traveling with clothes, but they're also hard to beat when it comes to consolidating the size of your closet (without getting rid of any precious possessions).

Although not as multipurpose or durable as garment bags, vacuum-seal storage bags can save serious closet space.

These wonder containers can shrink your stuff up to a quarter of its size. If you don't have access to a vacuum cleaner, don't fret—a little muscle goes a long way in squeezing out the air.

If you don't have a closet—tragically, some dorm rooms don't—look for a rolling rack. Invest in a sleek chrome variety, or give a standard a coat of playful paint. For something more modern, try a folding garment rack that opens up into an X shape.

If you have a closet without a door, set up a curtain rod to conceal your clothes with curtains.

## Garment Bags

- Garment bags are ideal for off-season clothes.

- They do more than simply save space. They can also be used to protect your fancier clothing and formal dresses.

- Dry-cleaning bags may be similar, but they make a poor substitute for garment bags. Canvas and nylon are preferable; avoid plastic altogether.

Less Stuff, More Space

- When it comes down to it, having less stuff is the key to having more space.

- Keep your drawers, shelves, and closet well edited. Don't keep things around unless they serve a real purpose.

- If you end up with lots of little-worn clothes, take a load to a local consignment store.

# CLOSET SHELVES
## Build closet shelves to boost vertical storage

Whether you have an actual closet or simply a separate armoire, your entire wardrobe will not be accommodated in your dorm closet. Make the most of the space you have with shelves.

Add to what the residence hall provides with hanging cubbies, compression corner units, and—most brilliant of all—stacking shelves.

Closet expanders, which hang from existing rods, add a second tier to any closet and will hold more clothes than you can even imagine. Similarly, hanging shelves can hold stacks of sweaters, heaps of T-shirts, and pairs of shoes.

Open storage cubes, available at organizing stores, rein in piles of folded shirts and sweaters and keep them from toppling over. The movable cubbies also provide support for the stacks on either side.

### Corner Shelving

- Corner shelves nest right into that neglected corner of your closet.

- Look for corner shelving that relies on spring tension to stay in place.

- Can't find anything in the home department? Shower corner shelves are sturdy enough to stash handbags, jewelry, and perfume bottles.

### Hanging Shelves

- While it takes up a bit of precious space on your closet rack, the vertical storage a hanging shelf provides is worth it.

- Make hanging shelves work for you. If you need extra space for your wardrobe, use the cubbies for stacks of sweaters and jeans.

- Shoes can be doubled up in the versatile cubbies and organized by dressiness.

Create a closet under your bed with short shelving units or salvaged drawers. Shelf dividers keep tall stacks from toppling over, and meticulous organization (by color, type, or frequency of wear) and labeling will keep your hidden-away clothes in heavy rotation.

**ZOOM**

Because your closet shelves have been used for more years than you can imagine, cover them and dresser drawers with slim cork or felt fabric. Carefully measure the length and width, then cut the material to fit. Not only will this protect your clothes, but it will add an unexpected pop of color.

## Tiered Shelves

- As long as your wardrobe isn't filled with floor-length dresses (college is all about individuality after all), slide a tiered shelf under your clothes rack.

- These racks can be used for shoes, sweaters, or anything you need extra space for.

- A shelf on wheels makes for even easier in and out, especially in a cramped, hard-to-navigate closet.

### Expanding Closet Shelves

- Plastic drawers can be stacked on top of closet shelves to increase the storage to the ceiling.

- Salvaged drawers can turn a top shelf into a storage unit. Store stacks of sweaters and towels and keep a stepladder around for easy access.

- Shelf dividers, rack doublers, and hanging shelves can be combined to make an incredibly space-efficient closet.

**DRESSING**

# ACCESSORIES
## Style is in the details; load up on accessories

When you're reaching for the same jeans and sneakers day after day, accessories matter. They can elevate even the simplest of outfits and put a personal stamp on basics like T-shirts, jeans, and sweatshirts.

It's important to build up an array of accessories—from belts to scarves to neckties—but it's even more essential to store a budding collection in a beneficial way. Accessories can easily fall to the wayside in an overflowing wardrobe, so display your add-ons as decor.

Dangling from hooks, fancy handbags make for a fabulous wall display. Ties can be draped from decorative clothesline or ribbon.

Wall hooks can hold (and flaunt) tons of accessories. Stuff unused purses and tote bags with scarves and sweaters for

### Accessory Racks

- Tiered accessory hangers can hold belts, scarves, and ties and be hung up right alongside clothes in a closet.

- Accessory hoops, a metal ring attached to a hanger, stows scarves, belts, and anything else that can be

  looped through the circle shape.

- Make your own accessory hangers with shower curtain hooks.

- Create a diamond (or two!) with wall hooks to hang accessories.

### Multipurpose Hangers

- Make the most of each hanger by using the hook as an accessory holder.

- Hang up clothes, as usual, and then dangle a corresponding belt, scarf, or tie around the hook.

- A traditional hanger can also be used for ties and scarves by draping them through the widest part of the hanger.

built-in storage. Painted in a bright color, a vintage hat rack can be a cool addition to any room.

A hanging toy chain from the kids' department will expertly hold accessories with ease. Installed from the ceiling, the chain will take up zero floor space.

If you'd rather conceal your accessories than display them, invest in a tie valet, belt hanger, or dandy accessory hooks. Consider draping belts and ties around the hangers of coordinating sweaters, shirts, and pants for no-fuss outfits in the morning.

## Belt Hangers

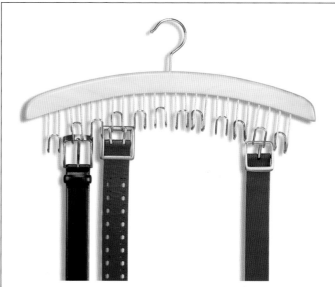

- Belt hangers take up the same amount of space as a traditional hanger, but they can hold up to fifteen belts.

- Buy two and use one to hold scarves, umbrellas, and other odds and ends.

- Make your own belt hanger using a classic wooden hanger and a handful of small screw hooks.

## Sewing Kits

- Even sewing novices can mend a hem or fix a loose button if properly prepared.

- Keep a small sewing kit on hand for clothing mishaps. A needle and neutral-colored thread are musts.

- Safety pins, straight pins, and pin cushions have a way of coming in handy when you least expect it.

- Double-sided tape allows for last minute hemming and missing-button fixes.

# JEWELRY
## Storing jewels, gems, and other sparkly extras

Since most students' uniforms for class consist of plain T-shirts, faded jeans, and their oldest pair of sneakers, the jewelry box might not get as much use as you'd expect. If your jewelry isn't going to be decorating you on a daily basis, why not use it to decorate your room?

Instead of hiding jewelry away in drawers, display it on hooks, fancy platters, and clever trays.

Tiered platters or multilayer cake plates can organize jewelry by color, dressiness, or wearability. Even elevated soap dishes display jewelry in an unexpectedly pretty way.

For stowing jewelry in drawers, compartmentalized kitchen items, like ice-cube trays and muffin tins, keep necklaces tangle free and earrings paired up. Small juice goblets or cocktail glasses can be lined up, side by side, to create separate

### Jewelry Hooks

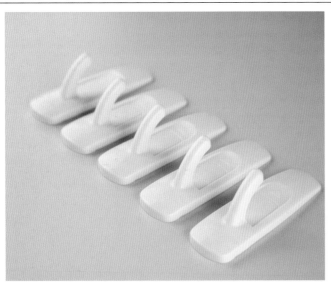

- Apply adhesive hooks to the walls, and group jewelry together to create wall decor.

- 3M makes teensy clear hooks that won't distract from the display of jewelry.

- For safekeeping and simple accessorizing, adhere hooks *inside* the closet

- If allowed, knock a row of nails into the wall and hang one necklace on each peg for a decoration that's as gorgeous as the jewelry.

### Jewelry Stands

- Stands are a way to store jewelry that might be more beautiful than the baubles themselves.

- T-shape stands can hold bracelets and necklaces.

- Similar to T-shape stands, jewelry "trees" can also store dangling earrings.

- Antique candy dishes hold tons of vintage-esque jewelry in the prettiest way.

cubbies for each piece of jewelry. Line the drawers you are using to store jewelry with felt or cork to minimize sliding.

A piece of pegboard and a handful of S hooks can parade your prettiest necklaces and dangling earrings. You can use upholstered panels or painted corkboard as well.

Hanging jewelry organizers, commonly known as jewelry rolls, sort and store jewelry in a simple, easy-to-travel way.

**ZOOM**

What kind of jewelry to bring to school? Everyday jewelry can stay in a decorative tray or pretty catch-all bowl, while costume jewelry should be stored in a drawer or used as decoration. Antique gems and heirloom jewels are better off at home.

## Jewelry Drawers

- Set aside a drawer or two to store jewelry and accessories.

- Keep everything organized with trays and boxes that are as compact as they are pretty.

- Fruit trays, egg holders, and tiny baking tins are the perfect size to stash bracelets, bangles, and chunky earrings.

- Silicone baking cups, which come in bright, playful colors, are an adorable way to store your earrings and hard-to-find jewelry.

### Safekeeping for Jewels

- Jewelry boxes are pretty, but small desktop drawers stow jewelry in a more inconspicuous way.

- Leave the expensive baubles at home. Diamonds, pearls, and any heirlooms that hold significance just aren't safe in a dorm.

- If you can't survive the semester without your beloved jewels, keep them in a discreet place, like in a small cloth pouch in the back of your desk drawer.

# SHOES

## From flats to flip-flops, sneakers to sandals, keep your college shoes in tip-top shape

Unless you're Imelda Marcos's great-granddaughter, you do not need one hundred pairs of shoes in your dorm room. Realistically speaking, you won't need more than ten. Most days will be spent in your comfiest pair of shoes—flip-flops or sneakers, depending on your style—and while occasions arise to dress up and trade your so-cozy-they-could-be-slippers shoes for *real* shoes, you won't need many (and you won't need them often).

Before you buy a storage container, think about how many shoes will be lying around your dorm room and how much space you'll have to work with.

Over-the-door pockets, which can stash between twelve

### Tiered Shoe Racks

- Pro: Racks keep shoes off the floor and in tip-top condition, and if kept neat, they really add some decorative value.

- Con: They put your shoes out in the open and on display, so your grubby sneakers will need to be stored somewhere else.

- Pro: They can be stacked and expanded—essential if your shoe collection tends to double in size every time you go shopping.

- Con: Although they take up valuable floor space, tiered shoe racks can be stashed under the bed.

### Over-the-Door Shoe Pockets

- Pro: If you own a lot of flats and flip-flops, you can squeeze a pair in each pocket, doubling the storage capacity.

- Con: Sneakers, heels, and clunky sandals demand a pocket per shoe.

- Pro: Because most over-the-door shoe pockets are limited to holding ten or so pairs, this storage unit might put a crimp in your shoe-buying habit.

- Con: Shoe pockets aren't expandable, so if you foresee buying shoes through the year, try a tiered rack.

and twenty pairs of shoes, keep your shoes visible and protected. If you don't have a door to devote to shoes, closet-rod cubbies are a similar storage unit that holds shoes in plain view and off the ground. Couple pairs together, or double up and keep four to a cubby.

For those who consider their shoes more than just, well, shoes, display the acquired collection creatively. Wall shelves make for a perfect heels display, while sneaker stockpiles are better off stacked vertically in clear shoeboxes.

**ZOOM**

How many shoes should you bring to college? Make sure you have a pair for every possible occasion. Dressy shoes for dates, professional flats for job interviews, casual kicks for class, athletic sneakers for hitting the gym. After that, lifestyle and personal style should come into play.

## Hanging Shoe Shelves

- Pro: Handy hanging shelves can store at least twenty pairs of shoes—and even more if you have tiny feet!

- Con: Hanging shelves can't be expanded, but if you have the extra space on your closet rack, you can add another unit.

- Pro: The cubbies can also be used to store stacks of clothes.

- Con: If you have a full closet to begin with, hanging shoe shelves take up valuable space.

## Rotating Shoe Tree

- Pro: For shoes that are as nice to look at as they are to wear, rotating shoe trees put them on display.

- Con: Shoes that *aren't* nice to look at have no place on a rotating shoe tree.

- Pro: Shoe trees hold up to twenty-five pairs of shoes and add a lovely boudoir sensibility to a dorm room.

- Con: Shoe trees might be the priciest shoe organization option—and the hardest to find (try boutique-supply stores).

# TRASH

## Taking out the trash: a task that's never done

You didn't think you wouldn't have to worry about trash now that you no longer live at home, did you? When you live in a dorm room, you'll be astounded at just how fast a trash can fills up, and it will be up to you—or your roommate, if you strike it lucky—to take care of it.

Unless you can come up with a deal, the trash will become a duel of who can outlast it the longest. A filled-to-the-brim trash can isn't a pretty sight, but an overflowing trash can is horrifying. Waiting too long to take out the trash makes finally taking the trash out even more unappealing. To make matters worse, it's a great way to attract unwelcome critters.

If your roommate neglects to notice that you're doing all of the dirty work—figuratively and literally speaking—confront the situation. If he or she continues to let the trash runneth

### Trash Cans

- Any old bin will suffice— we're just talking trash here. But lidded cans cover the trash and diminish stink.

- Foot-pedal openers and swing-top lids are cleaner and conveniently no-touch.

- If you don't like the look of traditional trash cans, consider using a lined tote bag or handled basket, which can be hung under your desk or inside your closet to save space.

- Small baskets and galvanized buckets make really slick trash cans.

### Trash Liners

- Self-dispensing trash bags eliminate the need for storage. Store the roll in the bottom of the trash can, and one bag dispenses after another much like tissues.

- Look for trash bags embedded with odor reducers.

If trash smell is an issue around your room, these might be worth the extra dollar.

- In a pinch, use plastic bags from the grocery store as your trash-can liner. *Anything* is better than nothing.

over, pick up the slack (through gritted teeth, if need be).

Don't ditch your leftover food in your dorm room, unless you don't mind catching whiffs of four-day-old takeout. Dorms should have a trash room on each floor for sizeable—and spoilable—waste.

If the stench from your trash can begins to overtake your dorm room, sprinkle a little baking soda in the bottom of the trash can, which will lessen odors much more effectively than using half a bottle of perfume.

## Recycling

- It isn't practical to keep recycling bins in your room—because, frankly, there just isn't *room* so opt for easy residence hall alternatives.

- Many dorms have community recycling bins where you can drop your glass, plastic, and cardboard containers.

- If your dorm doesn't have a recycling program, take it upon yourself to talk to an administrator to change that.

- Dorms have hundreds of residents who drink hundreds of bottles of water and eat hundreds of boxes of cereal (seriously!).

### Chore Checklist

- Create a list of the chores that need to be completed in your dorm room. Break it down by frequency: every few days, weekly, bi-weekly, and monthly.

- Prioritize. Sweeping the floor and dusting surfaces are weekly must-dos, while cleaning the fridge can be done once a month or so.

- Rotating chores will reduce your own housework and never leave you wondering when the last time the floor was swept.

- A simple list will do, but if you're computer savvy, create a schedule on a spreadsheet.

CLEANING

157

# FLOORS

## Making dorm floors shine like the top of the Chrysler building . . . kinda

Your floor will never sparkle as much as it does on the day you move in. Even if you sweep daily, mop weekly, and vacuum every time a crumb drops, a dorm-room floor accumulates a shocking amount of dust, dirt, and drips.

With an arsenal of mops, brooms, and vacuums, your dorm-room floor can be clean—on a regular basis. No matter how spotless it is, it will never be "so clean you could eat off the floor." Sorry, plates are non-negotiable.

With hardwood floors, all it really takes is a once-over with a broom every few days. Rugs can simply be given a good shake outside. Regardless of your flooring preference, a vacuum will come in handy.

### Brooms

- A simple broom may be all you need, especially if you just use accent rugs.

- A classic "shaker" broom runs about $4. Modern brooms with attachable dustpans keep dirt particles contained.

- If you don't have the storage space for a broom, look for a decorative broom. They make them in bright colors, floral prints, even polka-dotted patterns!

### Swiffers

- Swiffers are easy to use, easy to clean, easy to store. They can be used wet or dry and are equally effective both ways.

- To cut down on the amount of refill cloths you go through, wash them by hand with laundry detergent and reuse two or three times.

- Swiffers with extendable handles can clean hard-to-reach corners of your ceiling that probably haven't been touched in years.

Wall-to-wall carpet requires vacuuming, and oversize area rugs can also benefit from a good cleaning, so consider investing in a vacuum cleaner if your room touts either of these floor coverings. Many dorms have vacuums on hand for resident use, but if not, buy the smallest, most compact vacuum cleaner available.

## Mops

- Traditional mops and sponge mops are messy and rarely worth the hassle unless you're cleaning a large area (which you are, most likely, not).

- Steam mops are filled with water and dispense minimal fluid, making for an easy wash and dry.

- A mop really isn't necessary for a year in a dorm. If the floor is in need of some water action, dampen a rag and push it around the room with a broom—instant makeshift mop!

## Vacuums

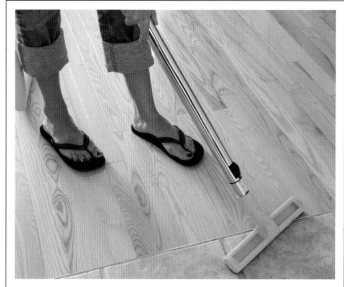

- Vacuums get rid of dust on hardwood and linoleum floors much more efficiently than a broom can.

- Vacuums are particularly good for people with allergies. Plus, a vacuum will always be useful in the future.

- Even so, you might not need to invest in a vacuum cleaner. Many dorms have vacuums for loan.

- Compact wet-and-dry vacuum combinations (Bissell makes a great one!) are convenient for small spaces, like dorms.

CLEANING

159

# DUST
## Banish dust bunnies from your dorm room with wise cleaning

Dusting is something you didn't pay much attention to before moving into the dorm, but it's crucial to pay attention to cleanliness while living in such a small space.

Most spray cleaners on the market are multipurpose, perfect for everything from wood to glass to plastic. Find one cleaning solution that can clean all your dorm room's surface areas—but check the label to be sure it's safe for everything first.

Stock up on a big container of cleaning solution when you first move in. To save serious space, buy a concentrated version that's intended to be diluted with tap water. One bottle should last an entire semester and will take up only a small bit of storage space.

Concentrate on multitasking cleaning supplies. Wipes eliminate the need to store tons of cleaning-supply bottles,

### Dust Busters

- Feather dusters mostly just move dust around, although authentic feathers and retractable brushes hold onto particles pretty well.

- Handheld vacuuming devices pick up dust pretty well, and if your room is small enough, you might be able to get away with this instead of a full-size vacuum cleaner.

- These small, powerful contraptions can also take care of spills, crumbs, and other day-to-day accidents,

- Even better, dust busters work on wet and dry messes.

### Dust Wands and Cloths

- Expandable wand dusters can hit hard-to-reach areas.

- No need to pay heaps of money for flashy "microfiber" dust rags. Even old T-shirts and towels work as dust cloths.

- A cool paper-towel holder can sit right on the desktop, always ready to help out with any spill.

and seeking out all-purpose cleaners reduces the number of cleaners you need to buy to begin with.

Make cleaning a weekly habit. Just a few minutes getting friendly with an all-purpose spray (there's not much it *can't* do) will dramatically improve the state of your dorm room.

An unexpected and brilliant dust buster can be found in your laundry basket; dryer sheets can remove the dust from computer monitors, TV screens, miniblinds, and fan blades.

## Dustpans

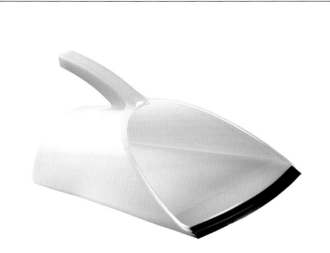

- A broom and dustpan are a powerful duo when it comes to cleaning your dorm room.

- Look for a dustpan that sits upright, and use it as a storage container for your cleaning products.

- No dustpan? A spare folder or even a piece of cardboard can scoop up swept-up dust with ease.

**Cleaning Dorm Room Rugs**

- Every few weeks, vacuum the rug and spot clean with stain remover.

- Have the rug professionally cleaned at the end of a semester and the year.

- Every few months, flip the area rug over and vacuum the bottom.

CLEANING

# SANITIZING
## Sanitizing your way to good health

Remember in elementary school when the common cold was a constant, sort of like coloring books and recess? Dorms are even more germ prone and cold friendly.

Freshen up your dorm room with fans, humidifiers, and those miraculous wall plug-in air fresheners. When the weather is nice (not too hot, not too cold), crack open the windows and reacquaint yourself with fresh air.

Sanitizers—both for hands and for surfaces—should be kept in high supply. With germs galore, regular once-overs with bacteria-busting cleaners are a must.

Buy a big container of hand sanitizer and squeeze it into a nice glass jar with a hand pump. This will look much nicer sitting on a desktop, and having such a pretty bottle in sight will serve as a reminder to rub some on every few hours.

### Fans and Humidifiers

- Give your nose a break! Humidifiers keep the dry dorm air moist and fresh, but they're a bit of an investment.

- Classic tabletop fans improve any room's air circulation without costing much money or taking up too much space.

- Oscillating fans keep the air moving, providing relief for overworked A/C units, and offer much-needed white noise in a loud residence hall.

### Air Purifiers

- Your dorm's air-conditioning unit will most likely date back to that old residence hall bed: In a word, it's *old*.

- Tabletop or floor air purifiers cost less than $100 and capture a roomful of dust, pollen, and other icky air impurities.

- The smaller, the better, so as not to take up too much space or disturb your decor scheme.

- Some companies make colorful modern purifiers that look more like art than air filters.

Hand sanitizer isn't a magical answer to avoiding germs; washing your hands—and everything those fingertips touch—is. That goes for your computer keys, your TV remote, your drawer handles, and most of all, your doorknobs.

## *Hand Sanitizers*

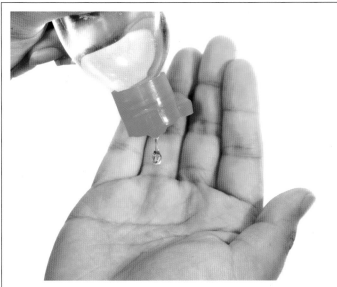

- Keep a bottle of hand sanitizer handy. One on your desk, one in your backpack, and one in your car isn't too much—it's nearly necessary.

- Nothing beats the convenience of the carry-everywhere container of sanitizer, but nothing beats the cleanliness of soap and water.

- Hand sanitizers are essentially alcohol, so combat the drying effects with a high-quality moisturizer.

## *Cleaning Cloths*

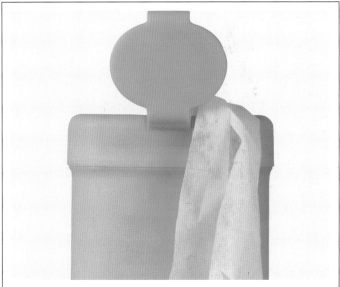

- Disinfecting wipes come in a canister for easy dispensing and spotless storage.

- They come premoistened, so you don't have to deal with spray cleaners and cloths.

- Whether using them as a sanitizer or disinfectant, simply wipe the surface. Sanitizing takes thirty seconds; disinfecting requires letting the solvent soak in for four minutes.

- A to-go package is perfect for carrying around in your tote.

CLEANING

# KITCHEN
## Make the most of your dorm's makeshift kitchenette

They say if you want something done right, you should do it yourself. Perhaps this old adage will make you feel better about the fact that you will be your best dishwasher in college.

Instead of dwelling on your newfound dishwasher-free existence, think about how great it is to have the luxury of a dining hall for many of your meals, and make the most of

hand-washing dishes by using delicious-smelling soap, soft hand towels, and lots of fun tableware.

Use a decorative container for dish soap, and opt for stylish dishtowels instead of hand-me-down cloths. If you're doing dishes in the bathroom, consider buying dish soap that can double as hand soap.

The best way to deal with filthy dishes is to prevent them

### Kitchen Soaps

- If you don't like the idea of a bottle of dish soap among your bath products, stash it in a sleek lotion dispenser.

- Buy concentrated dish soap so you only have to use a dab and only have to buy it half as often.

- Look for formulas with vitamin E and aloe, so they'll soften hands while they clean dishes.

### Dish Towels

- Whether you have an actual kitchen or not, keep a stack of dish towels handy.

- They're much more eco-friendly than paper towels and a heck of a lot more economical, too.

- Loop towels can hang anywhere and add serious style, especially if you can find retro patterns at your local vintage store.

from the beginning by keeping your food fresh with lidded containers and knowing just how long those leftovers have been in your refrigerator.

Instead of tacky Tupperware, look for sleek glass containers with snug lids. Not only are they nice enough to eat from or serve out of, they can stand in for storage containers, too. If glass makes you nervous, melamine dishware is meant for outdoor dining but might as well be made for dorm-dwelling students. It's cheap and unbreakable and comes in all sorts of cool prints.

## Storing Clean Dishes

- Paper plates and disposable containers may seem convenient, but classic dishes and canisters are much more ecofriendly.

- Buy a mishmash of vintage dishes and store them atop your desk—just stack them up layered with squares of felt in between.

- Compartmentalized plates and serving trays can double as desktop or in-drawer organizers.

## Cleaning Your Refrigerator

- Remove all the food from the fridge and check to see what's expired and can be thrown out. Take out any removable shelves and add-ons.

- Clean the inside with a soapy cloth (dish soap works!), and wipe completely with a clean, dry towel.

- For a finishing touch—and an odor remover—wipe down with a solution of one cup water and one tablespoon vinegar.

CLEANING

# LAUNDRY
## Mastering the washer and dryer away from home

Your least favorite experience of college won't be exams; it will, inevitably, be laundry. Don't feel intimidated by the task, though. As long as you stay on top of it, there's no need to buy double the underwear. It's easier than shopping and a lot more economical.

Store your laundry in a mobile hamper that can be carted to and from the laundry room or laundromat. Don't let it get too overstuffed, or you'll risk a trail of underwear to and from your room.

Fold your laundry as soon as it's clean—right out of the dryer, if possible—to prevent wrinkles. Because some wrinkles are inevitable, keep an iron on hand. If the thought of ironing laundry moves you to grab the cleanest shirt off your floor, just buy a big bottle of wrinkle releaser.

### Hampers

- Keep your clothes in a hamper—not on your floor. Make it easy on yourself by keeping a hamper near where you change clothes.

- Pop-up hampers make lugging laundry a cinch; even better is a sleek wooden frame with a removable canvas bag.

- If you want something that can stand in as decor *and* storage, colorful wicker is sturdy and stylish.

- Look for hampers with portability. You need to be able to lug it to and from the laundry room without spilling your undies all over the hallway floor.

### Laundry Detergents

- Laundry detergent is a personal preference. Ask Mom what she buys, and follow suit.

- Concentrated detergents allow you to use half the amount with all the cleaning power.

- Read the directions to see how much detergent is recommended per load; different brands call for different amounts.

- Don't forget dryer sheets, which help clothes retain softness.

Unless you have a hamper full of stained clothes, stick with cold water, which is easier on your clothes and a much more ecofriendly option. Detergent that's specifically formulated for cold water is very effective.

To green your laundry routine even more, look for eco-conscious laundry detergents. What sets them apart from traditional detergents is that green formulas contain organic fragrances, nontoxic solvents, natural stain removers, and biodegradable ingredients (and containers!).

## Drying Racks

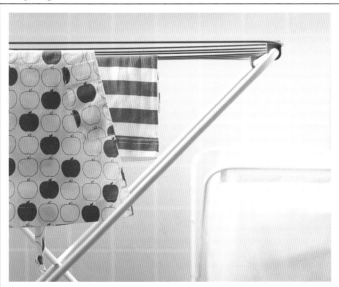

- Laundromats are known for their magical shrinking abilities.

- Can't fit into your jeans anymore? It's not you—it's the dryer.

- Consider air-drying denim, sweaters, and other delicates that may shrink in size.

- Another option? Instead of running the dryer for the full sixty minutes, check on your load after a half an hour or so.

## Ironing

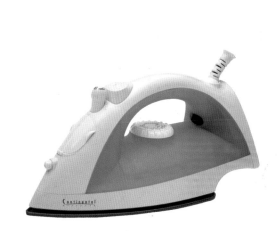

- An iron is one of those things that Mom will insist you need for college, and it will remain in the back of your closet all year long.

- Buy one, but look for the smallest model to save space.

- Bottled wrinkle releasers are effective. But, if you wear a lot of easily wrinkled clothing, they are not very economical.

- Make your own wrinkle releaser by combining water with a splash of fabric softener in a spray bottle.

CLEANING

# CREATING DECOR
## Get crafty: Who knew being cheap could be so stylish?

When it comes to do-it-yourself decor, think big and start small. Little projects like picture frames, dry-erase boards, and collaged corkboards will make a serious difference on the overall style of your room.

Decor is in the details. Give yourself a much-needed study break, and head to the local craft store to stock up on inexpensive additions that can fancy up equally cheap items around the room. You can paint frames and mirror borders bright colors, embellish them with jewels, cover them with fabric, and decoupage them with decorative paper.

If you have a few empty picture frames on hand, think outside the box (or inside the frame, rather). Turn an oversize antique find into a chalkboard or fasten on hooks to make a coat rack.

With a hot-glue gun, anything is possible. Attach rhinestones,

### Picture Frames

- Trim frames with colorful ribbons or ruffles. A few dots of craft glue can completely transform a dime-store frame.

- Buy a bag of jewels or sequins and bedazzle any frames that need a little extra shimmer.

- Even Popsicle-stick frames can look fancy with enough bling and bright paint.

- Look for frames that can do double duty, working on a desktop and walls alike.

### Curtains

- Sheets and tablecloths make instant curtains. The edges are already hemmed (often in the perfect width to slide onto a curtain rod).

- Don't fret if the edge of the curtain does not meet up the windowsill.

- Floor-dusting curtains actually make the ceilings seem higher and the room larger.

- Drapery clip rings will turn a sheet of fabric into a curtain without the need of a sewing machine—just clip on, and voilà!

studs, and silk flowers to anything that needs a little flair.

Spray-mount adhesive can turn wrapping paper into make-shift contact paper, which can be used to cover everything from frames to desk accessories to wall decor.

**ZOOM**

Make your own matching desk set with patterned fabric scraps and a can of Mod Podge. Cover picture frames, coffee cans, even a desk lamp with coordinating material, then use these cheery accessories to decorate your desktop.

## Message Boards

- Turn any surface into a dry-erase board with sheets of clear or white contact paper.

- Galvanized steel, found at any home-supply store, can make a simple and sleek magnetic board.

- Any surface can be painted with magnetic or dry-erase paint—just be sure not to coat anything that's owned by the school.

## Corkboards

- To make your own cork-board, purchase a piece of fiberboard and a sheet of cork.

- If they aren't the same size, simply trim the cork to fit the board with a sharp utility knife.

- Attach the cork to the fiberboard with heavy-duty glue, then lightly sand the edges.

- Decorate with ribbons, colorful tacks, and lots and lots of pictures, magazine cut-outs, and mementos.

CREATING

# CREATING SHELVING
## Keep looking up when it comes to dorm decorating

You have lots of stuff, so you need lots of storage. When you're living in a room as small as a closet, the key to maximizing your space is to look up—literally. Adding shelves and building vertically can turn empty walls into serious storage.

So what's a space-starved college student to do when most residence halls put the kibosh on installing shelves with screws and nails?

Old wooden ladders are a charming alternative to traditional tool kit–requiring wall shelves. With a few coats of paint, a ladder becomes a wonderful shelving unit complete with rungs that make the perfect showcase for your prettiest knickknacks.

Once you sand, paint, and decorate your ladder, you can no longer use it as an actual step stool. Keep in mind that paint

### Vintage Ladder

- Look for a ladder with flat steps that are at least three inches in width. Any hardware or home-supply store should have a selection of ladders for under $50.

- If you can't find one you like, making a ladder is a simple project that should take only a few 4 x 4s and an hour or two.

- Freestanding ladders—the variety that lean against a wall instead of unfolding into a double-sided step-ladder—are ideal.

### Sandpaper

- Lightly sand the entire ladder, from top to bottom. Concentrate on the edges, steps, and other splinter-prone spots.

- Because your ladder is soon to be used as a shelving unit, you'll want to remove any blemishes and chips.

- Once you've completely sanded the ladder, run a clean rag over it to catch any sharp edges.

hides potential rotting and damage, so be sure the ladder is steady before covering it.

If you can't get your hands on a full-size ladder, opt for a small step stool. It can double as a bookshelf or nightstand.

## Bright Paint

- Buy a can of paint and a quality one-inch paint-brush. Use a color you really like—this is the kind of piece you'll hold onto for years.

- Cover the ladder with one coat of semi-gloss paint, allow a few hours to dry, and then apply a second coat.

- Once completely dry, use fine sandpaper if you'd like your ladder to look distressed.

## The Final Product

- When your ladder is complete, lean it up against a wall in your dorm.

- Fill it with knickknacks, keepsakes, and anything else you would display on a shelf.

- If you need extra space for hanging, drill small hooks into the bottom side of a few ladder rungs.

- From those hooks you can dangle necklaces, medals, and other mementos.

171

CREATING

# CREATING FURNITURE
## Turning old into new and revamping vintage goods

An afternoon spent combing through thrift shops and garage sales can yield enough $5 furniture to furnish an entire dorm room. What these finds lack in luster, they make up for in potential. Just a little imagination and a few craft supplies can turn an ages-old nightstand or a beat-up side table into a one-of-a-kind gem.

Decoupage, which is essentially cutting and pasting to create an artsy collage, can be a unique and easy way to update old furniture.

Decoupaging with decorative paper—from scrapbook sheets to gift wrap—can be used to securely (and simply!) cover furniture with a bit of multipurpose spray adhesive. The beauty of decoupage is that you can use *anything* as a cover and you can cover *anything*.

## Secondhand Furniture

- Don't shy away from furniture that isn't in tip-top shape. Almost anything can be fixed up with a coat of paint or a bright piece of fabric.

- Wood is the easiest material to redo, because it's so simple to cover with a coat of paint. Remember to sand down any nicks and scratches.

- Look for nightstands, bookcases, small free-standing shelves—anything with a lot of personality *and* potential.

## Colorful Paint

- Bright paint breathes new life into old furniture. Retro chairs and tables look especially cool revamped in neon colors.

- Choose a paint that's playful, and don't be afraid to go with a color just because it coordinates with your decor scheme of the moment.

- Don't worry about long-term love. Furniture can always be repainted as your own personal aesthetics change.

- Spray paint can get into nooks and crannies with ease; paint cans come in handy for more substantial furniture.

Does the thought of decoupage take you back to second grade art class? If so, opt for a stylish shortcut, and cover a scratched-up surface or beat-up facade with colorfully patterned contact paper. Another easy option is a bright can of spray paint.

Instead of looking at the nicks and scratches of old furniture, focus on the potential. A shabby kitchen stool can become a snappy nightstand. Grandma's wicker bookshelf can double as a study desk.

## Mirrors and Hardware

- Covering a shabby surface with a shiny new mirror can turn hopeless hand-me-downs into fancy furniture.

- Secure the mirror to the surface with rubber cement.

- You can also do this with furniture that belongs to the residence hall—just skip the adhering step and simply set the mirror on the surface.

- Another fast fix-up? Simply swap the old hardware for fun new knobs and handles.

## Decoupage

- Turn any surface into a scrapbook with crafty—and cheap!—decoupage.

- Anything with a flat exterior is fair game. Use photos of friends, cut-outs from magazines, important mementos like birthday cards, and concert tickets.

- Decoupage mediums depend on the furniture's material; crafting glue works for smaller projects, while larger items call for acrylic polyurethane.

CREATING

# CREATING LIGHT
## Shining a little light on DIY lamps

Lose those blinding overhead lights and create ambiance with scene-setting lamps, paper lanterns, and strings of holiday lights.

Begin with a basic lamp base; think of it as a blank canvas, because the possibilities are truly endless. Buy a simple lamp shade, and embellish it with paint, rhinestones, ribbons, and anything else you can get your hands on. Even scrapbook

stickers and decorative paper can transform an unassuming lamp.

A boring metal desk lamp can be revived with a can of bright spray paint. Simply cover it with a quick coat of metal primer first, then decorate to your heart's content.

Festive holiday lights have the potential to do so much more than simply light up a Christmas tree. Use small plastic

### Lamp Bases

- Basic lamp bases typically run about $10. Ceramic and wood are the easiest to add a DIY spin to.

- If you're feeling crafty, decoupage with decorative paper and craft glue.

- Even the most outdated lamp base can look impossibly cool freshened up with a coat of paint and a new lamp shade.

### Holiday Lights

- With tiny adhesive hooks you can arrange holiday lights virtually anywhere.

- Consider trimming a window, lining the underside of the desk, or embellishing the underside of a lofted bed.

- Because most novelty light strings have very short cords, purchase an extension cord or power strip.

- Test for burnt-out bulbs before hanging the lights. Bulb testers can simplify this process if you plan on keeping the holiday lights up year-round.

hooks to create the shape of a headboard above your bed or a valance above your window.

Gather a bundle of lights and corral them in a basket or tin bucket, then use it as a bedside nightlight.

## Paper Lanterns

- Lanterns are easy to install. You just need a few 3M adhesive cord clips. Some lanterns even come with the cord kit, complete with a plug-in and bulb socket.

- The key to keeping it neat is to have the cord run down a corner, rather than a flat wall.

- Depending on where you want to hang it on the ceiling, an extension cord is a must in order to run it all the way down to an outlet.

- Also, remember to keep the bulb wattage low. Paper and heat are not a dorm-friendly mix.

## Lamp Shades

- Lamp shades are cheap and plentiful enough to decorate and swap out as you see fit.

- Make a pattern with paint—stripes, polka dots, even floral prints. Or, create clusters of little starbursts of light by hole-punching through the shade.

- Embellish with a hot glue gun. Add buttons, rhine-stones, or an assemblage of Grandma's brooches.

- An even easier option is taking a piece of ribbon and adding a border to the top and bottom of the shade.

CREATING

175

# CREATING SWEET DREAMS
## Turn a humble bunk into a fanciful bed

Turn a humble dorm bed into an impressive abode with the help of a whimsical canopy, a stack of cozy blankets, and a surplus of throw pillows.

Canopies couldn't be more perfect for a dorm room; they offer much-needed privacy when you're sharing a room. Stylish, cool, and devoid of any saccharine-sweet lace, these easy awnings are not your little sister's canopy.

Crafting a real canopy requires a bit more handiwork than creating a similarly impressive illusion with draping fabric.

Bed linens are surprisingly simple to put a personal stamp on. The plainest varieties are also the least expensive, and they can be dyed, puff painted, embellished with sequins, and trimmed in ribbons. If decorating something as large as a bedspread sounds daunting, start with a pillowcase.

### Hanging Canopies

- Canopies that hang from the ceiling make the biggest impact and provide the most privacy.

- Consider mosquito nets. Although this wispy sheer material doesn't provide much privacy, it adds loads of ambiance.

- Or course, you want to make sure that what you use to hang it can handle the weight. Nothing is worse than waking up to a fallen canopy on your face.

### Draping Canopies

- If you snag the bottom bunk, a draping canopy is as easy as tucking an extra sheet underneath the top mattress.

- For something a little more streamlined, buy a tension rod and set it up across your bed.

- Hang color-coordinated curtains from the rod, creating a bed nook of sorts.

## Pillows

- Making your own pillows is surprisingly simple. Take two same-size pieces of fabric and sew the seams together.

- Try vintage scarves, fancy cloth napkins, even old T-shirts.

- Fancy up a plain pillowcase with ribbons, stamps, and puff paint.

## Bed Linens

- Sewing two flat sheets together makes a sleek duvet cover; try two contrasting patterns, which creates a reversible variety.

- Embellish a basic comforter with iron-on patches and machine washable adornments.

- Tie-dye white or light sheets to match your room's decor scheme.

CREATING

177

# CREATING PRIVACY
## An unassuming 12 x 12 room becomes a fabulous abode

Did you fail home ec? Never fear. Sewing a set of curtains is easier than whipping up a packet of Easy Mac. All that's needed are a needle and thread and a big piece of fabric—no seamstress experience required.

Curtains can turn a humble cubby of clothes into a lovely closet. Don't worry about buying window linens to fit. A shower curtain is often the perfect size, and double-stick tape, iron-on tape, and liquid fabric adhesive can hem in an instant.

Twist in a tension rod wherever you want to create privacy and keep your clothes concealed. You can use this same tension rod trick to turn your under-the-bed area into a storage unit, too.

Insufficient closet? Oversize wardrobe? A rolling rack can be

### Curtains

### Rolling Racks

- Spring-loaded tension rods are easy to use and don't require any tools.

- A tension rod allows curtains to hang *anywhere*, from a closet to a bed frame to a, well, window.

- You don't even have to buy actual curtains. A funky shower curtain or even an extra flat sheet should suffice.

- An old rolling rack looks instantly stylish with a thick coat of vibrant paint.

- Clothes racks can be found for under $20, and are the kind of thing that will come in handy long after college.

- If your wardrobe is going to be exposed, keep things clean and organize by color.

a stylish solution. They can be found at supply stores, vintage shops, or online discounters.

Another way to break the space and bring a little privacy is to add a folding room divider, which can bring privacy when you want it and can be stashed when you don't.

## Room Dividers

- Room dividers are surprisingly simple to make. Just hinge together two or three panels of wood, fabric-covered screens, even shutters.

- The best thing about fold-up dividers is that they can be stowed under a bed or in a closet when not in use.

- Look for folding closet doors on clearance for an instant room divider.

## Underbed Storage

- Install casters on salvaged drawers for instant under-the-bed storage.

- These are infinitely more economical than plaster rolling drawers and look markedly more stylish to boot.

- If you can't track down leftover drawers, milk crates would work just as well.

- Sand away any nicks or splinters, and line the drawers with felt or colorful contact paper.

CREATING

# CALENDARS

## College is the fastest four years of your life; use a calendar to keep up with it

Time flies when you're having fun, so keeping a calendar close by is extraordinarily important during your action-packed years of college.

It's best to use one calendar to keep track of *everything*. Not only will this serve as a reminder for upcoming obligations, but it will be a detailed record-keeper of the past year, so when you need a freshman-year refresher, all it takes is a flip through the calendar. Think of it as journaling—without all the nostalgia and mushy reflection.

You can effectively use multiple calendars together. For example, a cell-phone calendar can be synced to a computer's calendar, so important dates will always be a click away. If

### Wall Calendars

- Pro: If your dorm room is your primary study spot, your to-dos will be in constant view.

- Con: If all your time in your dorm room is spent sleeping, consider a pocket calendar.

- Pro: A stylish wall calendar isn't just useful, it's decorative, too!

- Con: It takes up wall space that could otherwise be used for posters, art, and other decor.

### Desktop Calendars

- Pro: A desk calendar puts everything in easy view, so you know what day it is and what needs to be done.

- Con: It clutters your desktop and could serve as a distraction.

- Pro: A page-a-day desktop calendar will remind you of the date each morning.

- Con: A page-a-day desktop calendar is entertaining but not very efficient for keeping track of must-dos.

you want to be doubly organized, carry around a cell-phone calendar in combination with a daily planner—when you're that tuned in, you'll never miss an important date.

Digital calendars aren't for everyone. Traditional wall and desktop calendars welcome doodles and dates, scribbles and notes. Writing important meetings and memos by hand might help you to remember them.

Before you buy a calendar, make sure it fits with your personality and lifestyle. Choose something that you're enthusiastic about using on a daily basis.

## MAKE IT EASY

Turn an empty wall into an oversize calendar. Peek through school-supply stores for a teacher's desktop planner. Usually about the size of a large poster, these pads have an entire sheet devoted to each month with more than enough room for notes. Affix it to your wall with adhesive strips and decorate it to please.

### Computer Calendars

- Pro: A laptop calendar program keeps everything at your fingertips.

- Con: It's only convenient if you take your computer everywhere—sitting in the middle of class, you might be lost without it.

- Pro: An online-based calendar can be checked from any computer anywhere on campus.

- Con: This creates a great excuse to go online every few minutes if you're easily distracted.

### Cell-Phone Calendars

- Pro: Cell-phone calendars are convenient, because they're always on hand.

- Con: Don't rely on your phone as a primary calendar. Cell phones—which are frequently misplaced—aren't reliable enough to store important dates and essential obligations.

- Pro: Cell-phone calendars can be synced to your computer calendar.

- Con: Keeping a calendar on your cell might tempt you to text.

# PERSONAL ORGANIZERS
## Staying organized with a frenzied schedule

Balancing school with socializing and work with play requires an extra hour or two each day—or just extremely efficient personal organization.

Campus bookstores offer elaborate organizers, but all you really need is a small notebook, a stack of sticky notes, and a clear idea of what you need to do and when you need to do it. Easier said than done, right?

Sticky notes, labels, and flags make studying and staying organized impossibly easier. Take advantage of the variety of colors and shapes available to organize by subject or urgency or just to please the eye.

When it comes to keeping track of tasks, personal digital assistants (PDAs) and pocket organizers serve the same purpose, and each has its own appeal. PDAs, which exist mostly

### Sticky Notes

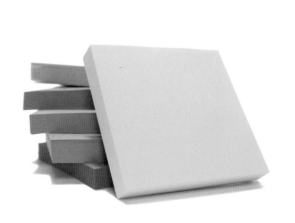

- Sticky index cards turn flash cards into an interactive activity—place them around the room and quiz yourself on foot.

- Color-coded notes, using a different color for each subject or project, get you instantly organized.

- In the middle of reading five different books? Use tacky tabs to keep your place and prioritize.

- These multipurpose stickies can also be used to flag important entries.

### Personal Digital Assistants

- PDAs are pretty much a thing of the past, but they live on as programs in smartphones.

- Word-processing software allows digital note taking equipped with computer syncing.

- Many universities rely heavily on e-mail, and PDA Internet capability makes it much easier to stay plugged in.

in the form of cell phones, eliminate the need for paper-and-pencil note taking and recordkeeping, but they're vulnerable to electronic malfunctions. Classic pocket organizers, like leather-bound Moleskines, are a convenient size and durable enough to throw in your bag.

## Pocket Organizers

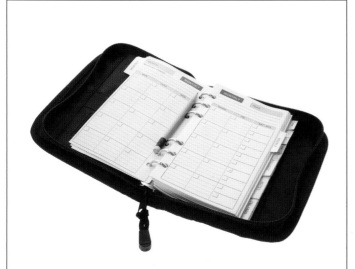

- Planners can be found in daily, weekly, monthly, and eighteen-month formats.

- Twelve-month planners are a standard, but many campus bookstores sell August-to-August notebooks—perfect for a student's schedule.

- Sometimes less is more. Left-brain thinkers might find it more beneficial to use an unlined notebook as a personal organizer.

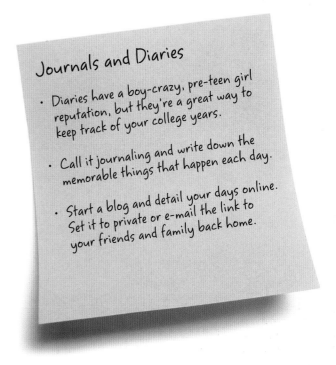

**Journals and Diaries**

- Diaries have a boy-crazy, pre-teen girl reputation, but they're a great way to keep track of your college years.

- Call it journaling and write down the memorable things that happen each day.

- Start a blog and detail your days online. Set it to private or e-mail the link to your friends and family back home.

# SCHEDULING
## Staying on top of your school and social schedule

Darting from class to work to study groups to exam reviews to club meetings to cafeteria dates can get exhausting—and can be impossible to keep track of.

Create an efficient schedule—and stick to it. If you have an understanding of exactly what needs to be done, and when, balancing school life with a social life is possible.

College students have a lot of unstructured time, so it's up to you to create a schedule. Don't sleep in until noon—just because you can!—when you could be getting a head start on an end-of-the-year exam.

Put your alarm clock to good use; get up at a reasonable hour. Factor in seven to eight hours of sleep (not more than that, and not too many less either). Sleek storage boxes or a filing system can keep all of your important papers and

### Packed and Ready to Go

- The best morning routine requires zero thought. With a prepacked backpack, go-to outfit, and on-the-go snack, getting out the door on time becomes a breeze.

- Know what you need to bring to class in advance,

so you aren't frantically running around your dorm room.

- If you keep textbooks and documents organized and ready to go, you'll never have to worry about running late to class.

### Wake Up . . .

- Sometimes waking up is the hardest part. No need to buy a separate clock radio just for the alarm; cell phones are well equipped with alarms *and* snooze functions.

- It may sound appealing—literally and idealistically—to wake up to your favorite

song, but some people only snap out of sleep with the more startling "ERRR! ERRR! ERRR!" of an old-fashioned alarm clock.

- If your alarm clock isn't working for you, take a look at your sleep schedule. The problem may be more than an ineffective alarm.

upcoming assignments within reach, even when you're running out the door.

Sometimes you won't get to do what you want, when you want. Perhaps all you want to do is sleep when you have a ten-page paper due in two hours. Sometimes coffee will be your best friend.

Organize your class schedule to make time for other things, like outside projects, after school jobs, and fun with friends.

**ZOOM**

Download widgets and applications for your laptop and cell phone that will put your schedule within a finger's click at all times. Calendars, to-do lists, and timers are all effective extras to keep you on task.

## . . . and Smell the Coffee

- Having a plethora of pick-me-ups on hand will help you work through those "I can't study another second!" moments.

- Easy access to a coffee-maker is crucial. A big mug of piping hot coffee is both comforting *and* energizing.

- The only way to study late into the night without droopy eyelids and spontaneous textbook snoozes is a stimulating music playlist. Oldies and hip-hop invoke head bopping and sing-alongs.

### Digitize Your Day

- Sync your cell phone, e-mail, and computer calendars together for optimal organization.

- BlackBerry smartphones and iPhones are immensely convenient in college because they keep important dates and school-related e-mails at your fingertips at all times.

- Always online? Gmail can integrate your calendar with e-mails, tasks, documents, and RSS feeds.

# ORGANIZING SYSTEMS

## Opt for an organizing system that simplifies your life

After being cooped up in high school for the entire school day, suddenly finding yourself with hours of free time can leave anyone a little wide-eyed. That's why developing an organizing system is crucial.

The system has to feel like a natural fit for you. If you're too caught up in "Getting Things Done" and can't seem to actually get your English take-home exam finished, it might not be worth the extra worry.

The key to a successful organizing system is that it works with your lifestyle and comes naturally. Add-on planners and calendars are perfect for über-organized students, while time-management systems, like the one described in the book, *Getting Things Done*, are more suited for creative minds who need a little structure and a lot of freedom.

### Day-Timer Calendars

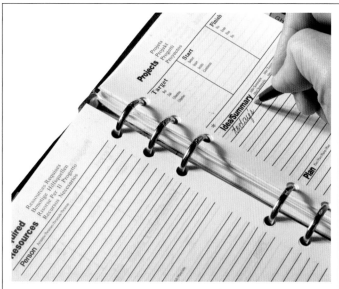

- Pro: You can create your own Day-Timer system, taking your own schedule and lifestyle into consideration.

- Con: Day-Timer calendars have so many options that it might be overwhelming to beginners in organization.

- Pro: The Green Series is the first organizing line to incorporate ecoconscious recycled materials in the planners and refills.

- Con: Day-Timer has been around so long, it might look a little antiquated to your young eyes.

### Getting Things Done

- Pro: Getting Things Done (GTD) is a method created by David Allen that recording to-dos externally frees the mind to focus on the task at hand.

- Con: GTD focuses on "control" and "perspective"—not prioritizing, which can be key to academic success.

- Pro: GTD principles don't require any additional products.

- Con: Until you get the hang of it, the GTD program can be more confusing than your actual tasks at hand.

No matter what organizing system you end up with—or if you forgo conventional "systems" for your own methodology—taking good notes is the first step to finding scholarly success. Write down everything, even the easy stuff.

While you're sitting in class, you might have a hard time understanding how you could possibly forget the date of an exam that the professor has underlined, circled, and highlighted to no end. But once you remove yourself from the classroom, all those reminders will disappear from your mind like cold pizza from the fridge.

**ZOOM**

Getting Things Done, which is basically "workflow for life," was launched in 2002. In 2005, *Wired* called it "a new cult for the info age." In 2007, *Time* magazine called the time-management program "the self-help business book of its time."

## The Franklin Planner

- Pro: Based around a simple three-ring binder, the Franklin Planner is about consolidating tasks, obligations, and appointments along with personal records in one place.

- Con: After the initial investment, Franklin Planners require additional inserts each year.

- Pro: The Franklin Planner eliminates the need for holding on to stray reminders and loose-leaf notes.

- Con: This hyper-organized system might not be conducive to a college student's spontaneous lifestyle.

**Create Your Own Organizing System**

- Keep track of syllabi, notes, and other important handouts by putting them in a designated folder or binder.

- Label, label, label. Specify which notebooks and binders should be taken to which classes. Tag the date and lecture that class notes are from.

- Know your schedule. If you have a handle on when your classes, meetings, and obligations are, you'll be able to factor in fun.

# PRODUCTIVITY
## Getting things done *now* means more time for fun later

There are scores of self-professed experts in the field of productivity, but finding a sweet spot of productivity has to come from within. Maybe you work better in the early morning hours with a piping mug of coffee in front of you. Maybe you work better after dinner, when you're well fed, well rested, and ready to knock things off your to-do list.

Staying organized is an easy way to stay on top of everything that needs to be done. Keep a running list of outstanding obligations, make a note of when everything is due, and cross things off as they are completed. The satisfaction of seeing everything that's already been completed will give you an extra push of productivity.

Whether you're trying to study during your roommate's marathon of *Star Trek,* or your neighbors are throwing a

### Organizing Desktops

- The key to a productive study session is having adequate space to spread out notes, textbooks, and index cards.

- An organized desktop makes studying that much easier. Clear off bills,

  magazines, books, and anything else that might be distracting.

- Stock up on school supplies. Highlighters, pens, pencils, and notebook paper should be readily available.

### Make a List

- A detailed list of everything that needs to be done will help you visualize a plan of attack.

- Be careful not to overplan. If adequate time isn't allotted for each task, a feeling

  of utter "woe is me" will inevitably set in.

- Don't write down general to-dos. If there's an upcoming history test, note exact concepts and details that need to be reviewed.

midnight dance party when you're catching some sorely needed beauty sleep, a nice pair of noise-canceling headphones will be music to your ears.

## Drown Out Distractions

- Slip on oversize headphones for instant peace and quiet.

- If music is as much a distraction as the roommate's incessant chattering, make a playlist with classical tunes or nature noises.

- Drowning out distractions does not mean blasting music. Be mindful of just how loud your tunes are—concentrated studying isn't worth losing hearing over.

### Find a Quiet Study Spot

- When distractions abound, seek alternative study spaces outside of your dorm room.

- Coffee shops near campus have a stimulating environment and provide an essential component for getting work done: caffeine.

- For demanding exams and taxing term papers, the campus library is invaluable. Surrounded by like-minded (and equally stressed) students, staying on task isn't as impossible.

# PROCRASTINATION

## Putting off studying, assignments, and obligations only worsens your workload

Procrastination is, at once, a college student's biggest enemy and greatest motivator. Nothing inspires quite like a looming deadline to get cranking on a chemistry paper; at the same time, cramming an assignment in the night before it's due will never result in the best work you can do.

It's easy to feel overwhelmed with a handful of outstanding assignments with rolling deadlines, but prioritizing will make everything seem much more doable.

The abundance of laptop-based homework has taken procrastination to a whole new level. With the prevalence of social-networking sites, entertaining blogs, and online games, finding yourself off task for an hour or two takes little

### Computer Procrastination

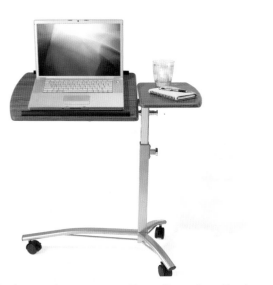

- Keep all other windows minimized while working on a paper—only the word document should be open.

- If the Internet isn't needed for online research, turn wi-fi off or unplug the cable.

- Turn off e-mail notification, close out instant message programs, and do *not* leave Facebook open.

### Old-Fashioned Procrastination

CHEMISTRY
PHYSICS
SOCIOLOGY
ASTRONOMY
BIOLOGY
SCIENCE

- Studying for five exams at once results in a whole lot of back and forth and not much learning.

- Put away unrelated textbooks and focus on the subject at hand. Out of sight, out of mind.

- Instead of trying to read a textbook from start to finish the night before an exam, condense important information on index cards.

more than a click away from your looming deadline.

Anytime concentration dwindles, social media sites have a way of taking over the computer screen.

Make a list of everything that needs to be accomplished. Create an agreement with yourself that an hour of work wins fifteen minutes of catching up on e-mail, scrolling through Facebook, or online shopping.

## MAKE IT EASY

Don't let friends enable your procrastination. When you're trying to get work done in your dorm room, wear oversize headphones to signal that you aren't available. Turn your phone off. Close out of instant messengers. Put a sign on the door that says, EARNING A'S, COME BACK LATER.

### *Study Timers*

- A kitchen timer works wonders when it comes to remaining on task. Set the timer to thirty minutes, and study intensely for short spurts of time.

- For assignments that require computers, download a desktop timer and use that to stay on track.

- A cell-phone timer works in a pinch, but this might prove too tempting for texting.

## Putting Off Procrastination

- The easiest way to battle procrastination is to avoid it altogether.

- Instead of waiting until the last possible minute to do the assignment, get started days (even a week!) in advance.

- The sooner you start an assignment, the easier it will be to complete. That doesn't mean you have to finish it as soon as you get it, but writing that first paragraph or figuring out that first answer from the start will make you far less apt to procrastinate.

# BUDGETING
## Maintain a college student's lifestyle with scrupulous budgeting

From the closet to the kitchen, small purchases and budget updates all add up. A sushi dinner here, a new sweater there; a movie ticket here, a new magazine there. All of a sudden you go from a savings account full of graduation gifts to a zero bank balance. When you go away to college, you're in charge of buying everything you need, and thus, you are in charge of keeping an eye on your spending.

Pay close attention to your "just this once" purchases. Maybe you don't buy *GQ* every month. Maybe you don't grab Starbucks every morning. Maybe you don't treat yourself to a nice dinner every night. But these "treats" wreak serious havoc on your bank statement.

Begin by identifying how you're spending money now—food? entertainment? clothing?—by writing down where

### Shopping Sprees

- Buying a new outfit for every occasion is a fast way to fall into debt . . . *and* run out of room in your closet.

- Avoid spur-of-the-moment shopping sprees. If you *really* need something, buy it—*after* you work it into your monthly budget.

- Be mindful of how much even the basics cost. When you're in college, go for the lower-end items. Once you've made your first million, splurge away.

### Eating Out

- After seven straight meals of dining hall food, the last thing you want is another cafeteria specialty ("meat" loaf, anyone?).

- Buying too many dinners away from campus can add up, especially if you and your friends frequent table-service restaurants.

- Dining out is an unnecessary expense when you have a college meal plan.

- Skip the daily Starbucks and splurge for a nice dinner once a month.

every dollar goes and what it goes toward purchasing.

Set goals that take into account your short- and long-term financial ambitions, then outline a budget that allows for all your monthly necessities, a few unexpected splurges, and future savings.

Closely track your expenses to make sure they stay within the guidelines you have set for yourself.

## *Entertainment on the Cheap*

- College towns are chock-full of cheap entertainment. Local bands sell concert tickets for less than the price of a CD.

- Many theaters will offer sneak previews. Call and ask how to get on the list; if all else fails, go to a matinee.

- A lot of campuses host movie nights, where they screen recent releases and new-to-DVD flicks—for free!

### Chic on the Cheap

- Dollar stores, yard sales, and Goodwill are a gold mine for unique, stylish finds. To uncover chic goodies for cheap prices, don't let any corner, shelf, or rack go uncovered.

- Don't be afraid to dig around, brush dust away, and envision what things might look like with a fresh coat of paint or new hardware.

- Dated patterns, chipping paint, and scratched surfaces can be refinished, recovered, and revitalized with a little creativity.

# BANKING
## Opening a local bank account boosts your financial freedom

Whether it's filled with $5 or $50, opening a savings account is the first step to full-fledged adulthood.

A bank is one of the safest places to keep your cash (especially when living in campus housing!). Talk to fellow students to find out where most people do their banking. Assess all your options. Are there national chains? On-campus locations? Multiple ATMs?

Buy two matching file folders: Use one for important schoolwork, like past tests and upcoming study sheets, and the other for essential financial documents.

If a parent is willing to cosign an account, joint banking gives your parents access to your finances, allowing them to add money, transfer funds online, and help you manage that ever-dwindling balance.

### Getting Started

- Choose between two basic bank accounts: checking and savings. Checking offers easy access but no interest; savings touts an interest rate with limited access.

- Be aware of fees for overdrafts, bounced checks, and dipping below the minimum balance.

- Put money back into your account regularly, even if it's just a few dollars here and there.

### Using a Checkbook

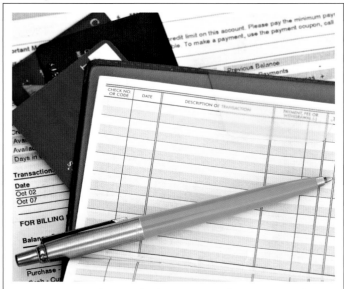

- Many students haven't had to write a check since they first learned how in junior high home ec.

- It's a simple fill-in-the-blank concept. Start by writing the date, then the name of the person or place that will receive the check.

- Write the numeral dollar amount in the small box. Then spell out that same amount, using words for whole dollar amounts and a fraction for amounts less than a dollar.

- Finally, sign off with your signature at the bottom of the check.

Most banks located in college towns are used to first-time customers and will be more than willing to brief you on the basics. But it is certainly helpful to go in with an idea of what you want to get from your first foray into banking.

········· YELLOW ● LIGHT ·········

Talk to your parents about finances *before* you get to college. There's nothing worse than borrowing money from friends for weeks on end, or worse, unexpectedly overdrawing your account. Find out if your parents are willing to give you a monthly allowance or put you on a budget for necessities.

## *Online Banking*

- Online banking allows instant access to deposits, withdrawals, and balances.

- Having a bank account at your fingertips eliminates the hassle of venturing out to the post office and mailing off your bills.

- Online banking is like finance for the Facebook generation. It's fast, easy, and on the go 24/7.

- More pros? Less paperwork, fewer fees, and, in some cases, higher interest rates.

### ATM Cards

- They're both shiny. They're both plastic. And they both seem like magic money. So what's the difference between credit cards and ATM cards?

- When you swipe your credit card, the purchase won't surface until your monthly bill comes, so you're spending money that you may not have. With an ATM card, the cost of the purchase is immediately removed from your bank account's balance.

- ATM cards can be used like credit cards to purchase things at stores, or they can be used at portals to take out cash.

- ATM fees add up. Find out exactly how many ATM portals are located near campus and where the closest one is. Can you get there by foot? By bike?

# CREDIT CARDS

## Charge it! Credit cards just might be a college student's lifeline and worst enemy

The summer before college, you'll probably receive several credit card applications—*a day*. By the time you move to college, approximately ten different credit card companies will contact you approximately three times with *almost* irresistible offers.

Credit cards have their merits. Not only are they incredibly convenient to carry around, but they essentially are money in your pocket. The key when it comes to credit cards is to only spend what you already *have*—and not money you anticipate earning.

The slippery slope starts when purchases are made with the assumption that money will sprout up on a tree next month

### Choosing a Credit Card

- Most credit card companies offer cards with perks tailored to college students.

- Look for "good behavior" rewards and "cash back" bonuses.

- Weigh the pros and cons of each card, and choose one based on your own lifestyle and income (or lack thereof).

### Saying "No" to Store Cards

- Every store you frequent is likely to offer you a retail credit card.

- Similar to any other plastic, this credit card allows you to charge anything—as long as it comes from said store.

- Because you're a college-age adult, salespeople will have no shame laying the pressure on to sign up for a store credit card.

- Store employees receive incentives for each application—whether they believe in the product or not—so be wary of these programs.

just in time to pay the bill.

If you choose to sign up for a credit card, keep it to one and stay on top of the balance. More credit cards mean more balances to keep tabs on and more bills to pay. Don't try to get away with just paying the minimum month after month, because eventually even the smallest amount will be too big to pay.

Look for a card with no annual fee and low interest rates, and if you can get a parent to cosign, even better! Not only will this raise your credit card limit, it will boost your credit score in the long run.

● ● ● ● ● ● ● ● ● ● ● ● ● ● ● RED ● LIGHT ● ● ● ● ● ● ● ● ● ● ● ● ● ● ●

A new law was just passed that doesn't allow people under the age of twenty-one to sign up for a credit card without a parental cosigner or a sufficient income to cover any potential debt.

## Building Credit

- Credit cards aren't inherently bad. In fact they're incredibly useful for building credit.

- Use your credit card regularly—and pay it off just as frequently.

- Establish checking and savings accounts and be careful not to overdraw either of them.

## When to "Cut" Back

- With its high interest rate, a college student cannot afford to have credit card debt.

- If the monthly bills become unmanageable, pay the balance and cut the credit card.

- If cash is too much of an inconvenience, ATM cards are a nice medium: They allow money withdrawals and "charges," but once you hit the end of your balance, the spending comes to a halt.

# FINANCIAL AID

## Getting help when it counts: Federal and academic financial aid makes learning more accessible

Scholarships and student loans can seem a bit like getting paid to attend college. They aren't, of course, but receiving a check in the month intended for school can be a great relief to students (and parents!) who aren't able to otherwise pay for four years of college.

There are three main types of financial aid: a *scholarship*

is financial support based on merit, a *student loan* is a sum of low-interest money lent for temporary use, and a *grant* is a federal fund intended for a specific purpose (in this case, education).

If your parents are willing to take on part of the financial burden, Parent Loans for Undergraduate Students (also

### Understanding Financial Aid

- Financial aid is a way for students to go to school, even if they can't afford it at the moment.

- Need-based financial aid is determined by guidelines set by the U.S. Department of Education and The Col-

lege Board, a not-for-profit association.

- Merit-based financial aid is determined by the donor of the scholarship—often times an alumni or company.

### Reading the Fine Print

- Know exactly how much you'll owe and when. If you can't enter the workforce after four years of college, factor that in the plan.

- Make sure you're aware exactly how much interest you'll accrue and whether you'll qualify for deferment.

- Read the fine print, and know exactly what's expected of you.

- Do loans include study abroad? Do they expect you to work? Do they offer state, federal, *and* private loans?

known as PLUS) lessen a student's post graduation debt and are often available at a much more reasonable interest rate.

Students who are footing their college education bill should stick with federal Stafford loans instead of private loans. While private loans are easier to get and much more openhanded as far as amounts go, the interest rates can be exorbitant and the legal protection is few and far between. Because Stafford and PLUS loans are federally funded programs, they're incredibly reliable.

## Earning Scholarships

- Apply to every scholarship that "applies" to you. There are scholarships for every niche group you can imagine: nationality, gender, region.

- There are many scholarships awarded for excellent grades or entrance test scores; there are even more scholarships available on a for-need basis.

- The key to earning scholarships is simply applying for them. The more you apply for, the more you'll score.

## Graduating Without Debt

- Is it possible to graduate without debt? Sure. Is it easy? Nope.

- The key to leaving school debt-free is to avoid loans, outstanding credit card balances, and overdrawn savings accounts—all easier said than done, of course.

- Debt isn't inevitable, but if you do end up with loans, kindly remind yourself that a college education is worth a few years of bills.

# SCRIMPING & SAVING

## Living big on less with the help of coupons, discounts, and pinching pennies

Pinching pennies is smart. Not smart in a nerdy way. Not smart in an impossible getting-an-A-in-chemistry way. Not even smart in a "I wish I could do *that*" way. It isn't hard to save money, it's just smart . . . in a clever way.

Sales, coupons, and smart shopping make all the difference when it comes to everyday purchases. Used textbooks can be up to half the price of new. Five sweatshirts can be snagged for the price of one at the end of the season. Even sodas can be found for free with the purchase of a deli sandwich.

So how do you find these deals? Look hard, shop often, and buy sparingly. Always assess the bargain racks before you splurge on brand-new goods. Always "pre-shop" online to

### Saving Money

- When it comes to saving money, every little bit counts. Do not skip necessities, but scrimp on luxuries.

- Be mindful of needs versus wants. *Need*: laundry detergent. *Want*: new jeans because your other pairs are dirty.

- Pooling your pocket change in a piggy bank will add up; use it as a rainy day fund.

- Make a list before you go shopping, whether you're heading to the grocery store or the mall. Stick with what you need.

### Coupons and Sales

- No one is too cool to use coupons, especially when they save you enough money to hit Starbucks a few extra times a week.

- The prevalence of savings Web sites makes the process even easier. Simply click, print, and save.

- Peruse the campus paper for local coupons, and national papers for chain-store savings.

see what's out there and what's on sale. And lastly, always think before you spend. Ask yourself, "Do I *really* need this?" even if you're just buying a bag of chips.

Mention the word *coupon* and you instantly picture an old lady with blue hair pulling out a stack of 5-cent coupons for store-brand soup cans. But coupons are an incredibly wise saving tactic for each and every generation.

Dollar-saving coupons can be found for haircuts, clothes, even nice dinners at fancy restaurants.

**ZOOM**

There are some really cool, vintage "piggy" banks that you can buy online these days, some that even have this whole dog-and-pony show go on when you insert the coin. Whatever gives you incentive to save even a pocket full of change is worth it.

## Student Discounts

**STANDARD IDENTIFICATION**

JANE A SAMPLE
456 ANYWHERE STREET
ANYTOWN, ANY STATE 99999

Expires 00-00-00

Sex: **F**     Hair: **Brn**
Ht: **5-05**     Wt: **120**
Eyes: **Blu**     DOB: **01-01-83**

IDENTIFICATION NO.
12345678

- Student discounts abound, especially in college towns.

- It never hurts to ask, so don't be shy to pull out your student ID, especially when you're dropping a significant amount of money.

- Some national restaurants and stores offer a 10 percent discount with a student ID.

### Garage Sales and Front-Stoop Finds

- Don't be afraid to barter. Oftentimes, a garage sale price is little more than a suggestion, and toward the end of the day, the seller will be willing to negotiate a deal.

- As a college student, focus on small decorative items (lamps, rugs, knickknacks) instead of big-ticket furniture.

- A $10 chair might sound like a steal, but if you don't have room for it, spend money on something you can actually use.

# FINDING A JOB

## The easiest way to leave college without a load of debt? Get a job

Attending school is a career in itself, but balancing academics with a job is possible. The ability to handle college employment depends on your class workload. If you're taking the minimum number of required hours, a part-time job will keep you busy without depleting your study time.

Know whether you're going to be looking for a job before you sign up for classes. Plan a school schedule that allows for downtime *and* work time by placing all your classes either on the same days (Tuesdays and Thursdays, for example) or during a specific time of day (from 9 a.m. to 1 p.m.). This will make you more employable while searching for a job, and you'll be able to accommodate taking on more hours once you land a position.

Need help with your résumé or interview skills? Go to your

### Be Professional

- When it comes to interviewing, trade your tennis shoes for heels and your sweats for a suit jacket.

- Whether you're applying at a clothing chain store or a prestigious local business, dressing professionally for the interview is a must.

- Not only does it instantly make you look more capable, but you'll never get a second chance at a first impression

### Perfecting a Résumé

- Drafting a flawless résumé is the first step to getting the job.

- A successful résumé reflects the personality and passions of the person it represents.

- No matter how well your interview goes, a great résumé leaves a lasting impression.

- Ask friends, parents, and professors to look over your résumé, and print it on professional cardstock.

school's career center. Advisers and employment experts offer advice for perfecting your appearance, both on paper and in person. Having a few experienced eyes glance over your résumé before you apply for jobs is invaluable. No matter how many times you proofread it, minor imperfections might go unnoticed until you get a fresh perspective from a helpful friend.

## Where to Work

- You can't afford to be too choosy, but you should have some say in where you work.

- Pay close attention to the hours, and let potential employers know you're a college student up front.

- These years are devoted to graduating college, so your work schedule should never interfere with preparing for exams or writing papers.

**Balancing Act**

- It becomes all too easy to get caught up in one area of life and let other priorities fall to the wayside.

- Don't let your academics get in the way of your friends, but at the same time, don't let socializing stall your studying.

- Use a calendar, daily planner, even a pocket-size notebook to keep your priorities in order.

# GYM TIME
## Penciling in the gym like you pencil in a date

Being an athlete in high school is sort of like getting an A on your times tables: Not everyone does it, but anyone who really wants to, can. Once in college, however, few people join organized sports teams, and many let their previous penchants for sports fall to the wayside. Time that was once spent running laps and lifting weights is suddenly replaced by video games and movie marathons.

Because many colleges include gym fees in quarterly bills, lack of funds is not an excuse *not* to work out.

Lack of time is a more plausible excuse, but even the busiest college students can squeeze in a few laps around the track or fifteen minutes on the elliptical.

Signing up for fitness classes will force you to fit exercise in. Buy an all-you-can-do pass, and stop by hour-long classes

### Weight Benches

- Lifting weights and building muscle increase your metabolism, keep your bones strong, and give you bursts of energy—all great assets for a college student.

- Start small and stick with simple weight routines—at least to begin with.

- If lifting free weights intimidates you, try starting with user-friendly machines or signing up for a training session.

- Start lifting weights when you're young, and make it a lifelong routine.

### Treadmills

- The quickest, easiest workout comes in the form of a treadmill. You can walk or run; you can stroll on an incline or on a flat level.

- Many campus gyms have modern treadmills that come programmed with workouts that you can personalize to your fitness level.

- Newer treadmills have individual TV screens and headphone jacks attached directly to the machine. Working out to an episode of your favorite show makes the time go by impossibly fast.

when you can. Taking a few yoga, Pilates, or weight-lifting classes will teach you the basics so you can continue to work out on your own schedule throughout the year.

The gym doesn't require fancy clothes, but make sure you come to college with adequate attire. For girls, that means supportive sports bras, simple T-shirts, and stretchy leggings or running shorts. Boys, stick with solid T-shirts and mesh shorts. Cross-training sneakers are well suited for any sport that catches your attention.

## Swimming Laps

- If you have access (and most students do), take advantage of the school's swim team lap pool.

- Alone time is impossible to find when you're living at a dorm—the solitude of a lap pool is incredibly relaxing.

- Fit in a few breaststrokes in between classes—just remember to buy a swimming cap to protect your locks.

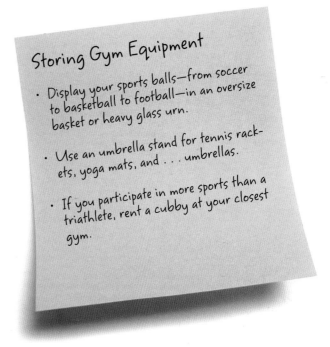

### Storing Gym Equipment

- Display your sports balls—from soccer to basketball to football—in an oversize basket or heavy glass urn.

- Use an umbrella stand for tennis rackets, yoga mats, and . . . umbrellas.

- If you participate in more sports than a triathlete, rent a cubby at your closest gym.

# FITNESS

## Make working out as routine as homework

Fitness is more than just going to the gym and pumping iron. Fitness can be taking a walk before class or doing yoga poses in your dorm room. Fitness can be throwing the football in the quad or shooting hoops on a street court.

No matter how you squeeze your exercise in, make sure you do *something*. It's too easy to be inactive in college: You're studying around the clock, you're sleeping less, and you're running on just a cup of coffee.

Maintaining a fitness routine makes it much easier to live a healthy lifestyle. It's okay to indulge in a midnight slice of pizza if you're going to be playing soccer tomorrow. It's okay to pound a few (*a few*—not ten!) energy drinks to get through a marathon of math if you're going to a yoga class in the morning.

### Get Moving

- Oftentimes the most challenging part of working out is changing your clothes and lacing up your tennis shoes.

- If going to the gym sounds as appealing as getting an F on an exam, look for exercise outside of the fitness center.

- Taking a walk around campus, exploring woodsy trails, or sauntering around the city can be counted as exercise.

### Exercising for Fun

- Round up a group of friends and hit the tennis court, football field, or basketball hoops.

- A pickup game should be no pressure and lots of fun. Recreational sports are a great way to sneak in exercise.

- If you used to be a sports star in high school, join an intramural league. Being part of an organized team guarantees weekly workouts.

Need an extra boost to hit the gym? Make sure your wardrobe is stocked with T-shirts, shorts, and socks that feel as good as they look. Keep your sneakers in fighting shape by padding them with insoles and replacing them every six months or so.

## ZOOM

Head to the library to find available workout DVDs. Many campus libraries have a movie section filled with a wide variety of every kind of video imaginable. Try beginner's yoga or Pilates, or pick up a versatile aerobics video. With fitness DVDs on hand, you can squeeze fitness into the day with just a few minutes of free time.

## *Exercising for Relaxation*

- Yoga and Pilates are perfect for students. These relaxing classes make you take the time to stop and exhale—something that's hard to do on the mile-a-minute college schedule.

- If you've practiced yoga before, keep a mat in your room for spur-of-the-moment downward dogs.

- If you haven't practiced yoga before, sign up for a few classes before trying it on your own (or with the assistance of a workout DVD).

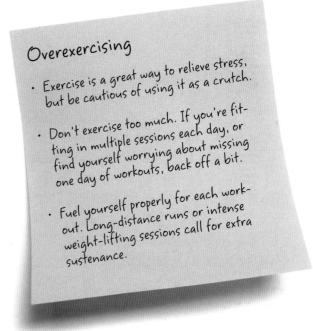

Overexercising

- Exercise is a great way to relieve stress, but be cautious of using it as a crutch.

- Don't exercise too much. If you're fitting in multiple sessions each day, or find yourself worrying about missing one day of workouts, back off a bit.

- Fuel yourself properly for each workout. Long-distance runs or intense weight-lifting sessions call for extra sustenance.

SURVIVING SCHOOL

# NUTRITION

Eating the colors of the rainbow—and we don't mean Skittles

Unless your roommate is studying dietetics, coming to college means not having anyone around to chide you for not eating your vegetables. Be aware of what you *should* be eating and why maintaining a well-balanced diet is important for more reasons than simply superficial.

Nutrition affects class performance, energy levels, and mental health as a whole. Fitting in five servings of fruits and vegetables each day will result in clearer skin *and* a clearer mind.

Occasional splurges and special treats are a welcome part of the college experience. It's always smart to have your health in mind, but don't pass up experiences (midnight pizza, ice-cream dates) because you're worried about your waist. Life is about striking a balance. Just like staying in to study tonight

## Healthy Snacks

- Snacking isn't inherently bad; it's only a problem when you reach for candy, chips, and other bites devoid of nutrition.

- Choose natural food over processed snacks. Fresh fruit over fruit snacks, a slice of cheese over Cheese-

its, an orange instead of orange soda.

- An arsenal of granola bars, individually packaged crackers, and other grab-and-go snacks will prevent you from getting too hungry and overeating at the cafeteria.

## Lots of Water

- Amid all your sodas, coffee, and energy drinks should be a healthy dose of nice natural water.

- If you don't care for the taste of your fountain's water, mix in a few drops of

fruit juice or invest in a purifier for your fridge.

- Aim for eight glasses a day to keep your energy up, your skin bright, and your body healthy.

means going to a party tomorrow, a sweet splurge today means a fresh salad tomorrow.

········· • GREEN ● LIGHT • ·········

Carry a sleek refillable water bottle around instead of going through three or four plastic containers each day. Make it a point to refill the bottle once every few hours, and you'll reach your water quota—in a very ecoconscious way!

## Sweet Treats

- It happens to all of us: Around 5 p.m. every day your energy plummets and all you want is a big chocolate chip cookie.

- Restore your vim and vigor—naturally—by reaching for, say, a piece of fruit instead of that cookie.

- Grab a snack that gives you that much-needed burst of energy without causing a sudden dive a few minutes later. Be wary of sweets and overly processed snacks.

### Eating Green, Local, and Organic

- Although it's admirable to eat entirely organic, it isn't easy as a college student.

- Instead, aim to eat as much local produce and organic packaged goods as possible.

- Ask around the cafeteria to find out what's organic and whom to talk with to get even more of a selection.

SURVIVING SCHOOL

# DIET
## Watching your waistline while living it up

Rest assured, the "Freshman Fifteen" is nothing more than a collegiate myth. Tales of greasy late-night pizza, cafeteria ice cream, and all-you-can-eat cheeseburgers? All true. But contrary to the common thought, the average freshman in college gains less than five pounds, making the "Freshman Fifteen" more like the "First-Year Five."

Maintaining a balanced diet and healthy exercise routine —and passing on seconds when the pizza box goes 'round— will keep your figure in shape and your precollege clothes fitting like the first time you wore them.

The key is to focus on good-for-you foods that also taste delicious. Eating salads for lunch and dinner might seem virtuous, but after a few days, meals will be monotonous to the point where you'll start to splurge spontaneously and

### Eat Breakfast

- There are no excuses not to eat breakfast. This wonder meal improves your class performance, increases energy, and gets your metabolism moving for the day.

- Break the fast with a nutritional breakfast, not just a cup of coffee or a glazed donut.

- If time is tight, grab a granola bar, banana covered with peanut butter, or yogurt topped with fruit.

### An Apple a Day

- An apple a day might not truly keep the doctor away (you're a smart college student, you already knew that . . . ), but apples are quite a wonder snack.

- Not only are apples cheap, they give your immune system a big boost with all their antioxidants, fiber, and vitamins.

- Make sure to get three or four servings of fruit each day. Apart from apples, grapes, oranges, and bananas are among the easiest to find—not to mention healthy, too!

overload on treats.

Small changes, like choosing veggie pizza over pepperoni and swapping mustard for mayo on a sub sandwich, really make a difference. Dieting is in the details: Choose water over sugar-filled drinks, opt for whole grains over refined white flour, and request sauces and dressings on the side.

•••••••••••••••• RED ● LIGHT ••••••••••••••

Crash dieting can be a miserable way to spend a few months at college. If you're struggling with weight, look into campus resources. Not only do they have specialists for eating disorders, they also have counselors who can help you find your healthiest weight.

*Freshman Fifteen*

- Don't become fanatical about weighing yourself; in fact, leave the scale at home.

- Instead, keep an eye on your weight by paying close attention to how your clothes fit.

- Watch the splurges. Instead of two scoops of ice cream, stick with one. Instead of a cookie with lunch and dinner, keep treats to once a day.

- Still drink filled-with-sugar soda? Replace it with fizzy water or hot tea.

## Healthy Thinking, Healthy Eating

- Eating nourishing foods and maintaining healthy habits will directly affect every area of your life, from classes to crushes, from grades to going out.

- Studies show that vitamin-filled foods have a huge impact on concentration, focus, and energy—all essential to earning great grades.

- Alternately, too much caffeine and sugar will deplete energy, turning a study session into naptime in seconds.

SURVIVING SCHOOL

# COMBATING COLDS
## Surviving cold season during the first year away at school

There's nothing like coming down with the sniffles for the first time while away from home. There's no real cure for the common cold, but remedies and treatments can put you back in tip-top shape in no time.

There are things you can do to keep yourself healthy. Eat right, get regular exercise, and manage stress to keep your immune system at its best to help you fight off any cold bug.

If you do catch something, think back to Mom's or Dad's favorite cure-all solutions. Never underestimate the power of lots of water, several mugs of piping hot tea, and a few bowls of chicken noodle soup.

When you're feeling well enough, go for a walk. Not only is the fresh air beneficial, but taking a breather away from the stresses of class and on-campus commotion will put you at ease.

### Eating Vitamins

- Consuming lots of wholesome foods can help combat colds and will make you feel better if you've already caught one.

- Load up on vitamin C by nibbling on fresh oranges, slurping tomato soup, and sipping fresh-squeezed juice.

- Fresh fruits and vegetables are worthwhile for more reasons than just vitamin C. Eating enough fiber will build up your immune system, warding off sickness.

### Taking Vitamins

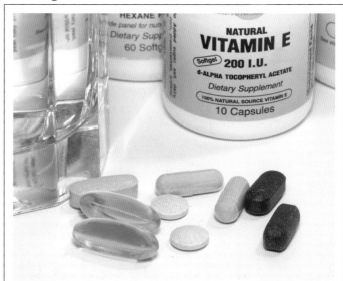

- Taking vitamins doesn't reduce the severity of a cold, but it does help to build up your immune system so you may avoid catching colds.

- Studies have shown that simply washing your hands might be more effective than taking vitamins, but the extra antioxidants can't hurt.

- Taking a multivitamin might be a good idea, since many college students have a different set of food groups than society as a whole.

Regardless of sickness, keep an eye on your vices. Smoking, drinking, and general college debauchery only make students more susceptible to contagious bugs.

Coupled with stress, allergies, and inadequate diets, a cold can make going to class difficult. Nip it in the bud with over-the-counter cold medication and hit up the doctor for a medical excuse if necessary.

## Treating Sore Throats

- Drink plenty of fluids to prevent dehydration: Water, tea, and juice are all great options.

- Dissolve a teaspoon of salt into warm water and gargle with the solution. Although this isn't the most enjoyable tactic, it noticeably reduces swelling and brings great relief.

- Buy a humidifier or vaporizer for your dorm room, or simply fill a shallow pan with water to filter moisture through the air as the water evaporates.

## Defense Against Germs

- Wash your hands several times throughout the day; when a sink isn't handy, a dab of antibacterial hand gel will do.

- Buy hand sanitizer in bulk and encourage friends and roommates to use it by placing it in a prominent spot.

- Spray disinfectant on desktops, doorknobs, dressers, and any other frequently used surfaces.

- Open the windows when the weather is nice; fresh air is a great way to get rid of germs.

# SURVIVING SICKNESS
## When you're under the weather away from home

Without Mom or Dad around, it's up to you to realize when you're sick. Before you chalk up a sore throat to last night's party or a bout of nausea to last night's meal, think about all your symptoms and don't think twice before calling a doctor.

As you were growing up, it's likely that your parents were the ones pushing you to seek medical attention and making doctor appointments for you. It's up to you now.

Going to a doctor's office is as painless as making an appointment. Medical numbers should be listed in your campus's student handbook, and doctors are likely to be flexible with your class schedule.

Take responsibility and understand that the sooner you feel better, the better your life—both socially and scholastically—will be. Another plus? Most doctors won't hesitate

### Doctor's Appointments

- A simple cold doesn't necessitate a visit to the doctor; anything slightly more serious does.

- Over-the-counter medicines can work wonders. Always stay stocked up on cough drops, ibuprofen, and cold medicine with a slight sedative (e.g., NyQuil, Tylenol P.M.).

- If a doctor gives you a prescription for medication, take it as prescribed. Many medications lose their effectiveness if not taken exactly as directed.

### Creature Comforts

- Do all the things you did when you stayed home sick from high school.

- Curl up on the couch (or, in a dorm's case, bed), watch fluffy movies, sip hot tea.

- Don't underestimate the healing power of a bowl of chicken noodle soup.

- Be mindful of your roommate. Don't toss your tissues around, and make sure to disinfect the door knobs, TV clickers, and high-traffic areas.

before writing a note that you can pass on to teachers for excused absences.

Exercise your best judgment when deciding whether to go to class. If you can meet your friends for lunch, you can go to class. If you can work out at the gym, you can go to class. If, however, you might pass out in the middle of campus, stay in bed and snag notes from a classmate.

## MAKE IT EASY

Make yourself a get well soon kit complete with green tea bags, vitamin C capsules, and travel tissues (to take to class!). When sickness hits and you can't muster up the energy to make it to the drugstore, these goodies will come to your rescue.

## *Getting Better*

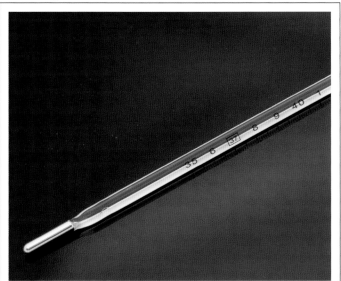

- Make it a point to take care of yourself—because, in college, no one will be around to nurse you to good health.

- Try to get in bed at a reasonable hour, drink lots of fluids, and take it easy. Basically do all the things your Mom and Dad implore you to do while home with a cold.

- Although college isn't quite as conducive to "sick days" as high school was, skip a class or two if need be.

### Campus Medical Plans

- Before you go to the doctor—or before you skip the doctor for fear of racking up charges—take a close look at your campus medical plan.

- Sometimes heath services are included in your general fees, which means a doctor visit will be virtually free.

- Always go to the doctor prepared with your student ID and an insurance card for maximum medical savings.

215

# ROOM LAYOUT
## Arranging a dorm room to accommodate all your collegiate needs

Changing the layout of the room can change the entire aesthetic of your space. The thought of rearranging might be daunting, but residence hall furniture is often conveniently on wheels or sliders, making room repositioning a cinch.

A clever arrangement will give both roommates their own individual spaces, maximize the floor space, and work with the room's inherent charm. Creating cubbies with furniture allows you to stash vacuums and trash cans out of sight.

The girls had different tastes when it came to decorating their dorm. Tessa loved bright colors and bold statement-making details, while Emilie leaned towards earth tones and hippie chic sensibilities. Because Emilie and Tessa were such good friends to begin with, they were very accommodating of their personal preferences when it came to color schemes,

### The Layout: Before

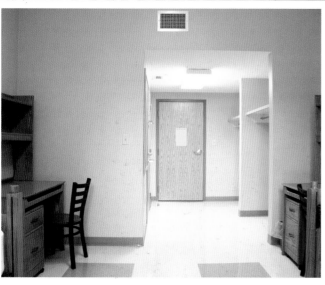

- Emilie and Tessa originally arranged their beds in an L shape.

- While this arrangement worked fine, the girls were sleeping head-to-head and had no room for bedside tables—or privacy.

- Setting the beds parallel brings a wonderful balance to a small dorm room and provides the perfect spot for a bedside table (with lots of storage).

### The Layout: Beds

- Instead of buying the exact same comforter as your roommate, opt for a coordinating color or pattern.

- Contrasting comforters can be tied together with coordinating pillows.

- Another option? Trade a decorative throw pillow with your roommate to create continuity.

wall decorations, and bedding.

As insignificant as it may seem, moving the dorm beds makes the single biggest impact. Bunked, the floor space is doubled. Lofted, the under-the-bed storage is amplified.

When it comes to under-the-bed storage, stick with color-coordinated drawers and brightly colored containers. If under-the-bed bins are both fashionable and functional, your clutter is concealed in style.

Regardless of the flooring, adding a cozy rug will turn a dorm room into a comfy lounge space.

## The Layout: Additions

- Using a windowsill as a storage area makes opening and closing blinds a big inconvenience.

- Adding a small table below the windowsill to hold text books, alarm clocks, and other bedside necessities prevents this.

- A bedside table doesn't have to be fancy. For Emilie and Tessa's room, we just used two sets of plastic drawers.

## The Layout: After

*The girls used their nicknames for design symmetry!*

- Parallel beds allow for more privacy than an L-shaped set-up.

- The between-the-bed floor space begs for a stack of fluffy floor pillows, perfect for a spur-of-the-moment movie night.

- Arranging desks on opposite walls allows for a quiet study spot for both roommates, because working back-to-back minimizes distractions.

- A rug turned cold linoleum into a plush floor. Cotton and wool rugs are equally cozy options.

DORM MAKEOVERS

# WALL TREATMENTS

Transforming white dorm walls with stylish decals, collages, and personalized decorations

Coming into the dorm room, Tessa and Emilie's walls were a bit haphazard. Think of dorm walls as a blank slate.

Corkboards dotted the walls in a checkerboard pattern. While small corkboards are a good idea, forming a solid focal point—like a rectangle, square, or diamond shape—creates a nice point of focus.

Emilie and Tessa personalized their walls with scrapbook paper–covered cardboard letters. Instead of spelling out their first names, they opted for nicknames. The girls used decorative scrapbook paper to cover their letters, but contact paper, gift wrap, and paint would also work well.

These handy press-on decorations are cheap, colorful, and,

KNACK DORM LIVING

## Dorm Walls

- Think of dorm room walls as the ultimate blank canvas. They're just begging for posters, corkboards, collages, and other decorative additions.

- Double-check with your residence hall rules before

- hanging anything up on your wall.

- Emilie and Tessa's dorm allows pins, but no screws, while other dorms on the same campus only allow 3M adhesives.

## Wall Decals

- Wall decals are fun *and* functional, and they essentially turn a wall into a life-size scrapbook.

- The set we found for Emilie and Tessa's room included frames and "pockets," which serve as catchalls for postcards and snapshots.

- Instead of covering the entire room with decals, choose one focal point.

- Before you slap on any stickers, make sure the label guarantees they are removable.

best of all, very residence hall–friendly. The best decals are as functional as they are fashionable. Many decals double as picture frames, and some serve as cubbies for concert tickets, college mementos, and flash cards for tomorrow's psych exam.

Although they have a reputation for being very "college," posters remain one of the best ways to decorate residence-hall walls. Just be choosy—don't collage your walls with every band and movie you've loved since the fifth grade.

## Corkboards

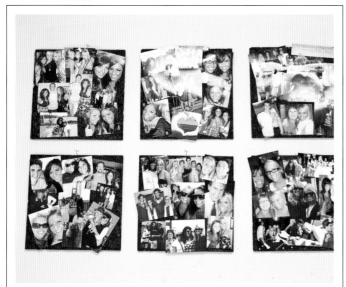

- Corkboards are a cheap and easy way to decorate a wall or two.

- Stock up on colorful, decorative pushpins, and beef up your photo collages with fancy paper and magazine cut-outs.

- Because they're so lightweight, corkboards can be attached with small pins or adhesive strips.

- Instead of dealing with one big bulky corkboard, a collection of smaller ones can be taken down and rearranged with ease.

## Personalized Letters

- Craft stores have all kinds of letters and shapes in DIY-friendly materials like foam and cardboard.

- Spell out anything from your nickname to your initials to inspirational notes.

- Decorate with paint, fabric, or decoupaged paper. In this case, each letter was decorated with contrasting patterns in a coordinating color scheme.

- These can be secured to the wall with adhesive strips or foam stickies from the craft store.

DORM MAKEOVERS

# WINDOW TREATMENTS

## Making the most of your (dorm) room with a view

Most dorm rooms come with very basic miniblinds, and while they make a fine foundation, they're as boring as your science textbook.

Emilie and Tessa's dorm room was outfitted with nice, new blinds. The blinds were rarely opened, though, because their windowsill doubled as a catchall surface for storage, holding music speakers, and picture frames among other things.

Adding a valance to the top of their window provided a little shade and a lot of style with minimal effort. Tension rods can be adjusted to fit the window width, so window treatments can be added without a tool box or elbow grease.

If opening and closing blinds throughout the day is too much of a hassle, hang full-length curtains and tie them back with ribbons when you want natural light.

### Dorm Window Treatments

### Valances

- The majority of dorm rooms come equipped with basic white blinds.

- If yours does not, consider investing in an inexpensive set. Blinds are convenient because they allow you to adjust the amount of light.

- Sheer chiffon panels are an even easier option, because they can be hung from a tension rod.

- Roman shades are a stylish and simple alternative to blinds, but most require mounting.

- A valance, which is decorative fabric at the top of a window, is a small addition that makes an instant difference.

- Valances are the perfect alternative if you don't want to deal with curtains but

still want to jazz up your dorm window.

- Choose a valance that ties both bed sets together. In this case, they chose brown, the unifying color for both bed schemes.

Curtains aren't just relegated to windows. Like Emilie and Tessa's room, many dorm closets are without doors, exposing haphazardly hung clothes and piles of dirty laundry. A tension rod can create a concealed closet with the help of an extra set of window curtains or, even easier, a shower curtain.

## Blinds

- Although they aren't the sleekest window coverings around, blinds provide privacy while still allowing for natural light.

- Keep the windowsill free of clutter to allow for easy opening and closing.

- Nothing looks worse than a jumbled half-open set of blinds.

- If the dorm-outfitted blinds are shabby, keep them pulled to the top and opt for curtains.

## Curtains

- Even if you don't want curtains for your window, consider adding them to a closet or under-the-bed area.

- Emilie and Tessa's doorless closet exposed all their clothes and clutter—not conducive to entertaining friends or concentrating on schoolwork.

- A tension rod and fabric shower curtain turned it into one of the most stylish areas of their room.

DORM MAKEOVERS

221

# BED
## Rest easy in an ecofriendly bed

When it comes to getting shut-eye, ecofriendly bed linens encourage a peaceful sleep. Don't assume that green products require more of the green stuff—all natural home goods often cost just as much as their synthetic counterparts.

"All natural" isn't synonymous with sleeping on hay. Although many options are derived from bamboo and hemp, they are every bit as comfortable (and in many cases, more so!) as

cotton. So what's the difference between the conventional cotton you've grown up with and its ecofriendly alternative?

Traditional bedding is made from conventional cotton, which is harvested using hazardous chemicals and insecticides. Not only are these harmful for the environment, they aren't too healthy to sleep with, either.

Organic cotton is not just less damaging to the environment

### Sheets

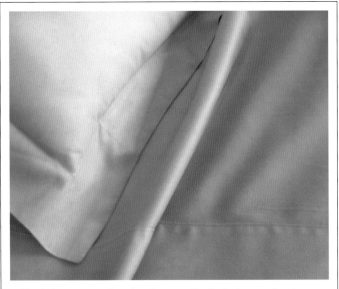

- Trade in your grade school synthetic sheets for a luxurious set of organic cotton.

- Bamboo sheets are far more comfortable than they sound. Even better, they're said to be more "breathable" than cotton.

- Similarly, hemp sheets are silky and soft—and incredibly energy-efficient.

- The price tag might be a little more expensive (expect to spend around $50), but the investment is worth it for a good conscience and a good night's sleep.

### Comforters

- Synthetic fabrics just aren't as comfortable as naturally derived materials like cotton and wool.

- In addition to being cozier to sleep under, ecofriendly comforters are more comfortable to hang out on, too.

- Buy gently used blankets or scour antique stores for vintage quilts.

- Secondhand shopping allows you to lessen your carbon footprint in style!

—it happens to be hypoallergenic, too. For even more incentive, organic cotton breathes well, encouraging quality sleep, and it's incredibly simple to care for (just toss it in the wash).

Organic wool is a natural insulator, making it ideal for keeping you warm in winter weather. Layer a wool blanket between your sheets and duvet for maximum warmth (and energy efficiency).

## Pillows

- Organic cotton is a fantastic option, but if you like your pillows firmer, look into hemp, which produces a soft pillow with a bit more bounce.

- Wool pillows are a firm and surprisingly soft option. Because the fabric wicks away moisture, you'll stay extra toasty.

- Believe it or not, one of the best green options comes from natural rubber. It creates a memory foam–like texture that's resistant to mold, mildew, and dust.

## Mattresses

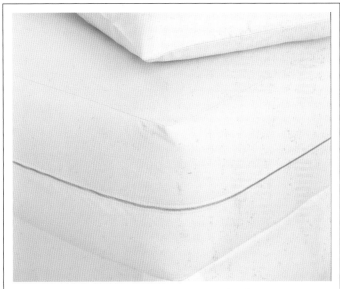

- Because you can't swap a dorm mattress for a fancy ecofriendly one, focus on buying a green mattress cover.

- Mattress pads extend the life of a mattress and will inspire peaceful shut-eye.

- Cover the dorm mattress with an organic cotton, wool, or latex pad to reduce contact with toxic mattress fillers.

- Allergy problems? Opt for a wool mattress pad, which happens to be hypoallergenic.

# BATH

## Cleaning yourself—and the environment—in one fell swoop

When you share a bathroom with a floor of other students and have to fight for a shower stall, being green probably isn't your top priority.

If your bathroom is located within a suite, you'll have more freedom to make your bathroom environmentally friendly. Ask the residence-hall coordinator whether the showerhead is a low-flow model, and if it isn't, swap it out just for the semester.

If possible, swap that icky PVC shower curtain for a non-vinyl alternative. The plastic material releases toxins into the air and has been linked to various health problems. Natural cotton and bamboo curtains are not only better for the bathroom, they look nicer and are easier to clean.

If you use a community bathroom, there's still so much you can do to make an impact. Try cutting your showers short,

### Showering

- It can be tempting to stay in the shower for hours when you don't have your little brother banging on the door.

- But it's a good idea to keep showers short; and don't leave the water running for more than a minute to let it warm up.

- Low-flow showerheads can cut water consumption in half.

- Organic bath products, like soap bars or two-in-one conditioning shampoos, are better for you *and* the environment.

### Drying Off

- Look for ecofriendly organic cotton and bamboo towels, which are suppler and softer than synthetic fabrics.

- Look for towels made with plant-based or low-impact dyes. These dyes create brilliant colors without doing any harm to the environment.

- Buy hand towels to use when you wash your hands, instead of reaching for a paper towel a few times a day.

- Look for the USDA Organic logo on the label for companies who go the extra mile to have their towels certified.

switching to all-natural soap, and turning off the faucet when you brush your teeth. Every little bit helps when it comes to living an environmentally conscious lifestyle.

Unplug any grooming devices—from hair flat irons to blow dryers to electric toothbrushes—after using. Simply switching them off isn't enough. Actually disconnecting the plug saves significant energy.

## Brushing Teeth

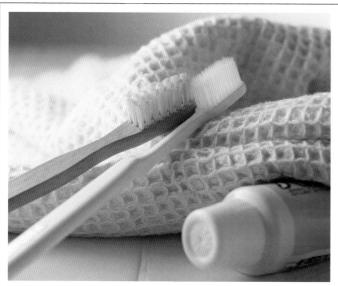

- To save serious water, turn off the faucet when you're brushing your teeth.

- Opt for natural toothpaste. As long as it carries the American Dental Association's seal of approval, it's just as effective.

- Toothbrushes with replaceable heads are economically and environmentally friendly.

- You can also find toothbrushes made completely from recyclable and renewable resources.

### Green Cleaning

- Chances are, you won't be in charge of cleaning your bathroom (definitely one of the best things about dorm living). But if you happen to find yourself with a need to clean, at least do it green!

- Looking closely at labels and opting for green cleaners over environmentally harmful chemicals is a small step that makes a huge difference.

- For an easy cleaner, mix baking soda with a drop or two of soap. Rinse off with water. This inexpensive and eco-friendly cleaner works in the bathroom and dorm room alike.

# LIGHTING

## Light up your room in an environmentally conscious glow

If your dorm room comes outfitted with halogen lights, there's not much you can do in the way of swapping the bulbs. What you can do is keep the overhead lighting to a minimum by furnishing your room (and setting the mood) with supplementary lamps equipped with ecofriendly light bulbs.

Before you buy a lamp, check the label to make sure that it can accommodate compact fluorescent lights (CFLs), which are much more environmentally-friendly light bulbs that provide light comparable to the incandescents you grew up using.

By definition, low-voltage lighting options, like CFLs, operate at 30 volts or less; classic light bulbs run on 120 volts. As if that alone isn't impressive enough, CFLs produce twice as much light as traditional incandescents.

Green lighting options are popping up on shelves by the

### Energy Efficient Lighting

- Watch out for the amount of time your lights are on. Turn them off before you leave the room, and never use them when natural light is an option.

- Using a lower wattage saves energy. If you can get away with a 45-watt bulb

instead of a 60-watt, go with the former.

- When the sun is down and the natural light is low, energy-efficient shades keep heat in during the winter and air conditioning in during the summer.

### Green Alternatives

- Solar panels charge by day and turn on at night. They provide about eight hours of illumination.

- Many solar-charged lights have a removable panel, providing a portable light source.

- Daylighting, which is essentially working in naturally well-lit rooms, has been shown to improve productivity.

day. Several companies make incredible LED lamps that provide up to eight hours of glow without the need for bulbs at all. These lamps work by charging on a luminescent base, and then can be removed to provide light anywhere you need it. Because they're portable, these lamps are perfect for late-night studying and in-bed reading.

Look into LED holiday lights, which last longer, burn brighter, and save more energy than their classic counterparts.

## Compact Fluorescent Lighting

- CFLs last up to ten times longer than typical incandescents.

- They use 75 percent less energy than a 60-watt incandescent and last up to ten times longer.

- Ideal for table lamps and task lighting, CFL bulbs create nearly 75 percent less heat, so they're a much safer option for the dorm.

- Incandescent bulbs generally last five hundred to two thousand hours. CFLs are guaranteed for eight thousand hours.

## Light-Emitting Diodes

- LED lightbulbs are a little pricier, but they last ten times longer than CFLs (60,000 hours!) and more than *one hundred times* longer than incandescents.

- LED bulbs may not be the most practical option for college students. One bulb can cost as much as $75.

- Skip the bulb and buy LED lamps, holiday lights, or light fixtures.

- LEDs come in multiple colors. White is best suited for indoor use, as it casts a soft white light without reflection, glare, or shadows.

GOING GREEN

# RESOURCES
## Decision-making made easy with the help of these additional sources

Planning for college includes making a lot of decisions—where to go, what to study, who to live with—but some decisions don't have to be difficult. With the help of this resource directory—which is in no way a complete list—you can now make educated decisions on your life, your living quarters, and your decorating schemes.

## Chapter 1: Choosing Your Dorm

**About.com College Life**
www.collegelife.about.com
Everything you need to know about college, from moving to dating to studying.

**Careers and Colleges**
www.careersandcolleges.com
Find scholarships, explore campuses, and research your dream colleges.

**Dorm Delicious**
www.dormdelicious.com
A fabulous dorm decorating resource from a fun collegiate viewpoint.

**Dorm Room**
http://dorm-room.com
One-stop shopping for dorm decor you never knew you needed.

**TheU**
www.theu.com
Virtually tour college campuses and read reviews from real students.

## Chapter 2: Moving In

**About.com Moving**
http://moving.about.com
Planning and preparing for your first big move.

**Moving.com**
www.moving.com
Find a mover or storage unit close to you, and don't miss the helpful guide to packing.

**Off to College**
www.offtocollege.com
A comprehensive college moving guide, plus tips about dorm living.

**UHaul**
www.uhaul.com
Great information about moving; particularly useful for cross-country traveling.

## Chapter 3: Rooming

**About.com Apartments**
www.apartments.about.com
How to deal with roommates and decorate rental properties (i.e. dorm rooms).

**Apartment Living**
http://living.apartments.com
Living and loving your new roommate.

### My Roommate Is Driving Me Crazy
www.myroommateisdrivingmecrazy.com
College survival tips about relationships, residential life, and roommates.

### Suite101 Student Housing
http://studenthousing.suite101.com
Student housing basics, from cooking in the dorm to choosing the right bedding.

## Chapter 4: Decorating

### Apartment Therapy
www.apartmenttherapy.com
A fantastic resource for decorating small spaces.

### Decor8
www.decor8blog.com
"Fresh finds for hip spaces," from the fingertips of a design whiz.

### Design Sponge
www.designspongeonline.com/
Easy DIY projects and inspiring before-and-after room makeovers.

### Making It Lovely
www.makingitlovely.com
Step-by-step directions for redecorating on a budget.

### Rental Decorating Digest
www.rentaldecorating.com
Temporary decorating ideas for residents who rent.

## Chapter 5: Furnishing

### Dorm Buys
www.dormbuys.com
Bed, bath, and furniture finds selected especially for dorm rooms.

### Ikea
www.ikea.com
Wallet-friendly furniture from the esteemed Scandinavian emporium.

### Pottery Barn Teen
www.pbteen.com
Although these home goods are aimed at teens, they're perfect for college students with a fondness for bright colors and funky patterns.

### Target
www.target.com
A great destination for cheap-and-chic home goods.

# Chapter 6: Sleeping

**College Bed Lofts**

www.collegebedlofts.com

Buy a bed loft instead of building one.

**The Company Store**

www.thecompanystore.com

Everything in home decor, with an emphasis on sheets, comforters, and bed covers.

**Dorm Suite Dorm**

www.dormsuitedorm.com

Dorm bed linens from the sweetly named online store.

**JCPenney**

www.jcpenney.com

The expansive home goods department has a wonderful decor selection geared towards teens.

# Chapter 7: Studying

**Cliffs Notes**

www.cliffsnotes.com

Brilliant homework shortcuts and exam hints.

**Lifehacker**

www.lifehacker.com

Personal productivity blog with tons of helpful downloads and Web applications.

**Spark Notes**

www.sparknotes.com

Study guides on a variety of academic subjects, especially literature.

**Student Hacks**

http://studenthacks.org

Learn how to "study smarter" with brain hacks and test skill tips.

**Zen Habits**

www.zenhabits.net

A laidback handbook about accomplishing more while stressing less.

# Chapter 8: Organizing

**The Container Store**

www.containerstore.com

How to organize everything from closets to cleaning products.

**HGTV**

www.hgtv.com

Decorating and organizing advice from TV's favorite home improvement channel.

**Organized Living**

www.organizedliving.com

College dorm essentials from purveyors of organization.

**Real Simple**

www.realsimple.com

Home decor and organization advice from the magazine that "makes life easier."

**Stacks and Stacks**

www.stacksandstacks.com

Stock up on storage, then ask their resident organizer any outstanding questions.

# Chapter 9: Entertaining

**About.com Entertaining**
www.entertaining.about.com
Every aspect of party planning, from etiquette to invitations to ice-breaker games.

**Better Homes and Gardens**
www.bhg.com
Lots of decorating ideas with a surplus of seasonal themes.

**Hostess Blog**
www.hostessblog.com
Explore a seemingly endless compilation of party themes complete with decorating ideas and recipes.

**Martha Stewart**
www.marthastewart.com
Learn to be an enthusiastic entertainer courtesy of Martha herself.

# Chapter 10: Eating

**101 Cookbooks**
www.101cookbooks.com
Delicious meals with an emphasis on simple and natural ingredients.

**Cooking Light**
www.cookinglight.com
Recipes that taste good and are good for you, too.

**Epicurious.com**
www.epicurious.com
From the publisher of *Bon Appétit*, this Web site has a huge selection of surprisingly simple recipes.

**TasteSpotting**
www.tastespotting.com
Hungry, but don't know what to eat? Scroll through this visually-tasty Web site.

# Chapter 11: Unwinding

**Zen College Life**
www.zencollegelife.com
Hack your way through exams, exercise, and self experimentation.

# Chapter 12: Bathing

**Bed Bath & Beyond**
www.bedbathandbeyond.com
Don't miss the college department filled with dorm-ready home goods.

# Chapter 13: Dressing

**Chictopia**
www.chictopia.com
Real people with really, really cool style.

**College Fashion**
www.collegefashion.net
Fashion advice for—and from!—college girls across the nation.

**Fab Sugar**
www.fabsugar.com
A wealth of fashion inspiration, both runway and real life.

### Who What Wear

www.whowhatwear.com

A daily dose of the best trends, plus tips and tricks about how to wear them.

## Chapter 14: Cleaning

### About.com Housekeeping

www.housekeeping.about.com

When mom isn't available, use this guide to answer any cleaning questions.

### UnClutterer

www.unclutterer.com

A blog about getting (and, more importantly, staying) organized.

## Chapter 15: Creating

### DIY Network

www.diynetwork.com

From the people behind HGTV, this is an invaluable resource for home (or dorm, rather) improvement projects.

### Do It Yourself

www.diyideas.com

From crafting headboards to building shelves, these step-by-step projects are simple and stylish.

## Chapter 16: Managing Your Time

### 43 Folders

www.43folders.com

Learn to make the most of your life, from mental sweeps to modest changes.

### Dumb Little Man

www.dumblittleman.com

Become a smart big man (or woman!) with this intelligent personal development site.

### Hack College

www.hackcollege.com

Clever shortcuts to make school socially and academically easier.

### Stepcase Lifehack

www.lifehack.org

Simple advice about productivity with podcasts, polls, and happiness plans.

## Chapter 17: Managing Your Money

### Fast Web

www.fastweb.com

Search for scholarships, find financial aid, and catch up on interesting news for college students.

### FinAid!

www.finaid.org

Calculate college costs, learn about financial aid applications, and browse through hundreds of scholarships.

**Get Rich Slowly**

www.getrichslowly.org

Named the "most inspiring money blog" by *Money* magazine, frugality and finance in a no-nonsense manner.

**Sallie Mae**

www.salliemae.com

Applications for student loans, both federal and personal, plus information about post-grad debt.

**Scholarships.com**

www.scholarships.com

Loans, grants, and fellowships, plus inspiring scholarship success stories from college students.

# Chapter 18: Surviving School

**College Confidential**

www.collegeconfidential.com

Search for colleges, find out about the admission process, and "ask the dean" your pressing questions.

**College.Gov**

www.college.gov

Cool college site from the U.S. Department of Education.

**Half of Us**

www.halfofus.com

Emotional health information with college students in mind.

**Inside College**

www.insidecollege.com

Over 700 lists of colleges by topic (for example, "Colleges for the Most Fun-Loving" and "Colleges for Students Slow to Make Friends").

**Surviving College Life**

www.survivingcollegelife.com

Definitive guide to college written by a recent graduate.

# Chapter 19: Dorm Makeovers

**Crate & Barrel**

www.crateandbarrel.com

Colorful rugs and pillows at a variety of price points.

**Target**

www.target.com

One-stop shopping for bedding, room decor, and cleaning supplies.

**Wallcandy**

www.wallcandyarts.com

From patterned ABCs to chalkboard animals, wall decals to suit anyone's style.

# Chapter 20: Going Green

**The Daily Green**

www.thedailygreen.com

Learn to be an environmentally responsible consumer and lead an ecofriendly life.

**Ideal Bite**

www.idealbite.com

A cheerful guide to all things green, from fashion to food.

**Re-Nest**

www.re-nest.com

Green living, with an emphasis on home decorating.

# ADDITIONAL READING

*1001 Things Every College Student Needs to Know: (Like Buying Your Books Before Exams Start)* by Harry H. Harrison Jr.

*Been There, Should've Done That: 995 Tips for Making the Most of College* by Suzette Tyler

*The College Dorm Survival Guide: How to Survive and Thrive in Your New Home Away from Home* by Julia DeVillers

*The Dorm Room Diet: The 8-Step Program for Creating a Healthy Lifestyle Plan That Really Works* by Daphne Oz

*Everything You Need to Know Before College: A Student's Survival Guide* by Matthew Paul Turner

*Getting Ready for College: Everything You Need to Know Before You Go From Bike Locks to Laundry Baskets, Financial Aid to Health Care* by Polly Berent

*A Girl's Guide to College: Making the Most of the Best Four Years of Your Life* by Traci Maynigo

*The Healthy College Cookbook* by Alexandra Nimetz

*How to Win at College: Surprising Secrets for Success from the Country's Top Students* by Cal Newport

*The Naked Roommate: And 107 Other Issues You Might Run Into in College* by Harlan Cohen

*The Smart Student's Guide to Healthy Living: How to Survive Stress, Late Nights, and the College Cafeteria* by M. J. Smith

*U Chic: The College Girl's Guide to Everything* by Christie Garton

*Worst-Case Scenario Survival Handbook: College* by Jennifer Worick

# GEAR CHECKLISTS

## FOR THE DORM ROOM:

❑ Bed lifts: Increase your underbed storage by giving your bed a bit of a height boost.

❑ Desk lamp: An additional light is a necessity for late night studying.

❑ Plastic drawers: Storage bins provide easy organizing for your extra stuff.

❑ Posters: Add personality to the cheerless white walls.

❑ Throw blanket: Ward off chilly winter drafts with an extra cozy layer.

❑ Throw rug: Cover up the linoleum with something soft and stylish.

## FOR THE BATHROOM:

❑ Bathrobe: Keep yourself covered to and from the shower.

❑ Oversized towel: Dry off in a shower stall as speedy as possible.

❑ Shower caddy: The easiest way to drag all your favorite bath products down the hall.

❑ Shower shoes: Protect those footsies from icky fungus.

## FOR THE CLASSROOM:

❑ Backpack: A sturdy bag is a must for all of your schoolbooks.

❑ Daily planner: Keep track of all your assignments, exams, and obligations.

❑ Multi-subject notebook: Instead of toting multiple ones around, invest in one big multi-subject notebook.

❑ Travel mug: Skip the cafe and bring your own coffee.

# GLOSSARY

**Adhesive Strips:** 3M has created an entire collection made with dorm-friendly adhesives. From hooks to poster hangers to spring-loaded clips.

**Armoire:** Also known as a wardrobe, armoires are occasionally used in lieu of closets in dorm rooms.

**Bath Caddies:** Plastic crates used to tote bath products to and from the community shower.

**Bed Lifts:** Plastic contraptions that lift a dorm room bed, providing at least five extra inches of underbed storage.

**Blackboard:** "E-learning" software that is used on many campuses across the country.

**Charging Station:** An electronic storage space that allows you to charge all of your devices—iPod, cell phone, camera—in one hub.

**Decoupage:** Decorating a surface by crafting a collage from cutouts, photographs, and other adornments.

**Down Comforter:** A soft fabric shell traditionally stuffed with fluffy goose or duck down.

**Dust Ruffle:** This piece of fabric that runs along the bottom of a bed is also known as a bed skirt. It's often used for decorative purposes, but also keeps dust from collecting underneath the bed.

**Duvet Cover:** Similar to the way a pillowcase covers a pillow, a duvet cover encases a duvet, allowing for easy laundering.

**Early Decision:** By applying early decision, a student indicates that a university is his or her top choice and is bound to that school if accepted.

**Ethernet:** Although most colleges have campus-wide wireless, some still use dial-up Internet that requires an Ethernet cord to gain access to the Web.

**Fifteen-Minute Rule:** If a professor doesn't show up within 15 minutes of when class is supposed to start, most universities give students the go-ahead to leave.

**Freshman Fifteen:** The purported weight that college freshmen gain, often blamed on a proclivity for late-night pizzas.

**Futon:** A configurable wood or metal frame topped with a mattress pad that can be used as a bed or couch.

**Getting Things Done:** Often abbreviated as GTD, this is a well-regarded time management system that's been known to boost productivity.

**Hand Vac:** Perfect for a dorm room, these small, portable vacuums clean up spills and freshen up floors with ease.

**Humidifier:** Small household appliance that increases the moisture in the air, which is particularly useful for older dorms.

**Lap Desk:** A portable surface that stands in as a desk, allowing homework to be completed on a dorm bed or common room couch.

**Mattress Pad:** A fabric layer that goes underneath the sheets, protecting your mattress—while protecting you *from* your mattress.

**Prerequisite:** A handful of fundamental classes must be completed before students begin upper-level courses in their emphasis area.

**Reading Day:** The last day of the semester before the week of final exams begins is intended to be a day when students can catch up on reading. On many campuses, it is also an excuse to throw a party.

**Resident Assistant:** Also known as RAs, these are upperclassmen students who supervise dorm residents.

**Syllabus Week:** For the first week of classes each semester, professors do little more than pass out and explain their syllabi.

**Time Management:** Managing skills, techniques, and time with a goal of maximizing personal productivity.

**Wellies:** Another name for rain boots, these are a must for storms that downpour minutes before you're heading to class.

**XL sheets:** You can buy sheets that are specifically designed for extra-long dorm beds, but many residence halls will tell students that regular twin sheets work. Listen to them—classic twin sheets are far cheaper.

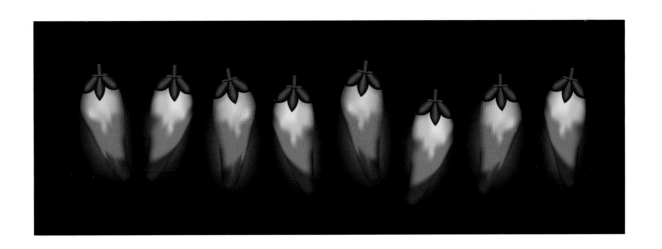

# PHOTO CREDITS

112 (left): © Lbarn | Dreamstime.com; 112 (right): © Robyn Mackenzie | Dreamstime.com; 113 (left): © Ken Toh | Dreamstime.com; 114 (left): © Chiyacat | Dreamstime.com; 114 (right): Courtesy of Ikea; 115 (left): © Andres Rodriguez | Dreamstime.com; 115 (right): © Robyn Mackenzie | Dreamstime.com; 116 (left): © Yvonne Bogdanski | Dreamstime.com; 116 (right): © Beachlane | Dreamstime.com; 117 (left): © Shaday365 | Dreamstime.com; 117 (right): © Greg Gerber | Dreamstime.com; 118 (left): Courtesy of Rubbermaid; 118 (right): © Jam4travel | Dreamstime.com; 119 (left): © Gregory Johnston | Dreamstime.com; 119 (right): © Daniela Spyropoulou | Dreamstime.com **Chapter 11**: 120 (left): © Ilja Masik | Dreamstime.com; 120 (right): © John Takai | Dreamstime.com; 121 (left): © Amy Walters | Dreamstime.com; 122 (left): © Eutoch | Dreamstime.com; 122 (right): Courtesy of Redbox; 123 (left): © James Steidl | Dreamstime.com; 124 (left): © Adisa | Dreamstime.com; 124 (right): Courtesy of Brookstone; 125 (left): © Kaarsten | Dreamstime.com; 125 (right): © Aleksandar Jocic | Dreamstime.com; 126 (left): © Alf75 | Dreamstime.com; 126 (right): © Arekmalang | Dreamstime.com; 127 (left): © Robert Kneschke | Dreamstime.com; 128 (left): Courtesy of PRshots/Very.co.uk; 128 (right): Courtesy of Ikea; 129 (left): © Eric Inghels | Dreamstime.com; 130 (left): © Ptlee | Dreamstime.com; 130 (right): © Jacus | Dreamstime.com; 131 (left): © Bert Folsom | Dreamstime.com **Chapter 12:** 132 (left): © Eutoch | Dreamstime.com; 132 (right): © Dana Bartekoske Heinemann | Dreamstime.com; 133 (left): © Roman Kalashnikov | Dreamstime.com; 134 (left): Courtesy of PRshots/Matalan; 134 (right): Courtesy of Bed Bath & Beyond; 135 (left): © Nicole Weiss | Dreamstime.com; 136 (left): Courtesy of Bed Bath & Beyond; 136 (right): © Christineg | Dreamstime.com; 137 (left): © ALEXANDER V EVSTAFYEV | shutterstock; 138 (left): Courtesy of The Container Store; 138 (right): Courtesy of The Container Store; 139 (left): Courtesy of Bed Bath & Beyond; 140 (left): Courtesy of Bed Bath & Beyond; 140 (right): © Steve Cukrov | Dreamstime.com; 141 (left): Courtesy of The Container Store; 142 (left): Courtesy of Oxygenics; 142 (right): Courtesy of Brookstone; 143 (left): © Chan Yee Kee | Dreamstime.com; 143 (right): © Pamela Tekiel | Dreamstime.com **Chapter 13**: 144 (left): Courtesy of Photos.com; 144 (right): © Pees | Dreamstime.com; 145 (left): Courtesy of Stacks and Stacks; 145 (right): Courtesy of Stacks and Stacks; 146 (left): © Tomasz Trojanowski | Shutterstock; 147 (left): © Spirokwok | Dreamstime.com; 147 (right): © Tomasz Trojanowski | Shutterstock; 148 (left): Courtesy of The Container Store; 148 (right): © Igor Terekhov | Dreamstime.com; 149 (left): Courtesy of The Container Store; 150 (left): Courtesy of The Container Store; 150 (right): © Radist | Dreamstime.com; 151 (left): Courtesy of The Container Store; 151 (right): © Anke Van Wyk | Dreamstime.com; 152 (left): © Onion | Dreamstime.com; 152 (right): Courtesy of Stacks and Stacks; 153 (left): Courtesy of The Container Store; 154 (left): Courtesy of Bed Bath & Beyond; 154 (right): Courtesy of Jill A. Fox; 155 (left): Courtesy of Stacks and Stacks; 155 (right): Courtesy of Stacks and Stacks **Chapter 14:** 156 (left): Courtesy of Ikea; 156 (right): © Birgit Reitz-hofmann | Dreamstime.com; 157 (left): Courtesy of Gaiam; 158 (left): Courtesy of Photos.com; 158 (right): Photographed by Mark Davidson; 159 (left): Courtesy of Photos.com; 159 (right): © Daniel Krylov | Dreamstime.com; 160 (left): © Igor Lovrinovic | Dreamstime.com; 160 (right): © Irina Iglina | Dreamstime.com; 161 (left): Courtesy of The Container Store; 162 (left): Courtesy of Bed Bath & Beyond; 162 (right): Courtesy of Brookstone; 163 (left): © Mingwei Chan | Dreamstime.com; 163 (right): © Ekaterina Bochkova | Dreamstime.com; 164 (left): © Kelpfish | Dreamstime.com; 164 (right): © Joe Gough | Dreamstime.com; 165 (left): © Aleksei Potov | shutterstock; 166 (left): Courtesy of Ikea; 166 (right): © Teekaygee | Dreamstime.com; 167 (left): Courtesy of Ikea; 167 (right): Courtesy of www.dormbuys.com **Chapter 15:** 168 (left): © Hannamariah | shutterstock; 168 (right): Courtesy of Ikea; 169 (left): © Raymond Kasprzak | shutterstock; 169 (right): © Petr Jilek | shutterstock; 170 (left): © stocksnapp | shutterstock; 170 (right): © bogdan ionescu | shutterstock; 171 (left): ©

Yobro10 | Dreamstime.com; 171 (right): Courtesy of Stacks and Stacks; 172 (left): © Igor Lovrinovic | Dreamstime.com; 172 (right): © John Holst | shutterstock; 173 (left): © Stephanie Swartz | Dreamstime.com; 173 (right): © Maroš Markovic | shutterstock; 174 (left): © Marilyn Zelinsky-Syarto; 174 (right): © Anne Kitzman | Dreamstime.com; 175 (left): © nick vangopoulos | shutterstock; 175 (right): © Nael_pictures | Dreamstime.com; 176 (left): © Adisa | Dreamstime.com; 176 (right): © Steve Bromberg Photography 2008; 177 (left): © Christoph Weihs | Dreamstime.com; 177 (right): Courtesy of PRshots/Matalan; 178 (left): © Zbieg2001 | Dreamstime.com; 178 (right): © William Wang | Dreamstime.com; 179 (left): Courtesy of Ikea; 179 (right): © Blueee | Dreamstime.com **Chapter 16:** 180 (left): © Miflippo | Dreamstime.com; 180 (right): © Newlight | Dreamstime.com; 181 (left): Lisa Wilder; 181 (right): © Nobody You Know | Dreamstime.com; 182 (left): © Olga Bogatyrenko | Dreamstime.com; 182 (right): © Iulius Costache | Dreamstime.com; 183 (left): © Newlight | Dreamstime.com; 184 (left): © Dmitry Bomshtein | Dreamstime.com; 184 (right): © Iwona joanna Rajszczak | Dreamstime.com; 185 (left): © Christian Draghici | Dreamstime.com; 186 (left): © Ragsac19 | Dreamstime.com; 186 (right): © Icefields | Dreamstime.com; 187 (left): © Tamas | Dreamstime.com; 188 (left): © Violet Star | Dreamstime.com; 188 (right): © DUSAN ZIDAR | shutterstock; 189 (left): © Aleksandar Ljesic | Dreamstime.com; 190 (left): Courtesy of Brookstone; 190 (right): © Graça Victoria | Dreamstime.com; 191 (left): © Birgit Reitz-hofmann | Dreamstime.com **Chapter 17:** 192 (left): © Elena Elisseeva | Dreamstime.com; 192 (right): © Kgelati1 | Dreamstime.com; 193 (left): © Pedro Nogueira | Dreamstime.com; 194 (left): © Scott Maxwell | Dreamstime.com; 194 (right): © Stephaniefrey | Dreamstime.com; 195 (left): © Otnaydur | Dreamstime.com; 196 (left): © Kati Neudert | Dreamstime.com; 196 (right): © Dmitriy Shironosov | Dreamstime.com; 197 (left): © Viatcheslav | Dreamstime.com; 197 (right): © James Steidl | Dreamstime.com; 198 (left): © Melanie Kintz | Dreamstime.com; 198 (right): © Milos Jokic | Dreamstime.com; 199 (left): © Ieva Geneviciene | Dreamstime.com; 199 (right): © Michael Ciranni | Dreamstime.com; 200 (left): © Cammeraydave | Dreamstime.com; 200 (right): © Graça Victoria | Dreamstime.com; 201 (left): © Aloysius Patrimonio | Dreamstime.com; 202 (left): © Jamalludin Bin Abu Seman Din | Dreamstime.com; 202 (right): © Javarman | Dreamstime.com; 203 (left): © Ron Chapple Studios | Dreamstime.com **Chapter 18:** 204 (left): © Frank Boston | Dreamstime.com; 204 (right): © Corlett050 | Dreamstime.com; 205 (left): © Angie Westre | Dreamstime.com; 206 (left): © Willian Quadros Da Silva | Dreamstime.com; 206 (right): © Lisa F. Young | Dreamstime.com; 207 (left): © Elena Ray | Dreamstime.com; 208 (left): © Paulpaladin | Dreamstime.com; 208 (right): © Muriel Lasure | Shutterstock; 209 (left): © Katarina Tilholm | Dreamstime.com; 210 (left): © Oliver Suckling | Dreamstime.com; 210 (right): © Brad Calkins | Dreamstime.com; 211 (left): © Kalina Vova | Dreamstime.com; 212 (left): © Craig Allsop | Dreamstime.com; 212 (right): © Bethany Brawn | Dreamstime.com; 213 (left): © Sydney Van Rensburg | Dreamstime.com; 213 (right): © Batuque | Dreamstime.com; 214 (left): © Zsolt Mate | Dreamstime.com; 214 (right): © Ron Chapple Studios | Dreamstime.com; 215 (left): © Kai Zhang | Dreamstime.com **Chapter 19:** 216 (left): Courtesy of Jill A. Fox; 216 (right): Courtesy of Jill A. Fox; 217 (left): Courtesy of Jill A. Fox; 217 (right): Courtesy of Jill A. Fox; 218 (left): Courtesy of Jill A. Fox; 218 (right): Courtesy of Jill A. Fox; 219 (left): Courtesy of Jill A. Fox; 219 (right): Courtesy of Jill A. Fox; 220 (left): Courtesy of Jill A. Fox; 220 (right): Courtesy of Jill A. Fox; 221 (left): Courtesy of Jill A. Fox; 221 (right): Courtesy of Jill A. Fox; 222 (left): Courtesy of Coyuchi; 222 (right): © Shutterstock; 223 (left): Courtesy of The Company Store; 223 (right): Courtesy of The Company Store; 224 (left): © Marek Tihelka | istockphoto; 224 (right): Courtesy of VivaTerra; 225 (left): © Liuyang | Dreamstime.com ; 226 (left): Courtesy of Knoend; 226 (right): Courtesy of Natural Collection; 227 (left): Courtesy of Bulbs.com; 227 (right): Courtesy of Vessel Inc.

# INDEX

INDEX

INDEX